# Ninja Creami

## Recipe Book for Beginners

1500-Day Ninja Foodi Creami Recipes Will Help You Transform Everyday Ingredients into Ice Cream, Gelato, Smoothie Bowls, Milkshakes, and More

**Ethel Bonnett**

# Table of Contents

# Introduction

Ice-creams and sorbets taste better when made with love at home. With the use of fresh and quality ingredients, your made homemade cannot only taste better, but it will be healthier than the ice-cream bought from the markets. And Ninja Creami provides you with an excellent option to make your ice-creams just the way you like it. There are several functions that this machine can perform to give your ice-creams and sorbet the perfect creamy or icy texture you would like. Ever since I laid my hand on my Ninja Creami appliance, I have never stopped making ice-cream for my family. Today, I have tons of recipe ideas that I have personally tried in the Ninja Creami, and through the text of this cookbook, I am going to show you how!

# Fundamentals of Ninja Creami

## What Is the Ninja Creami?

First, let's define Ninja Creami. With Ninja Creami, you can create a variety of frozen delicacies, including ice cream, sorbet, smoothie bowls, gelato, and milkshakes. It is extremely evident from Ninja that this is not a blender but rather a device that uses "creamify" technology to transform frozen foods into ice cream delicacies. In addition to having seven features, the CREAMi also employs proprietary "creamify" technology. To produce an ice cream with a smooth and creamy consistency, the CREAMi's blades cut through a solid block of frozen components. This implies that you freeze the custard base itself and the CREAMi transforms the already-frozen ingredients into ice cream instead of freezing your ice cream maker's bowl and chilling the custard that will make the ice cream. Therefore, just like a conventional ice cream maker, you will need to prepare the custard or other base in advance; it should freeze for at least a day, but ideally for 24 hours. That said, the CREAMi only needs a few minutes to do its magic because the components are already frozen. It takes only approximately five minutes to prepare compared to the typical ice cream maker's 15 to 20 minutes.

You might be curious as to what the Ninja CREAMi performs and how it functions. The Ninja CREAMi ice cream maker operates differently from conventional ice cream makers, as was stated in the review's introduction. The first step is to freeze the materials in one of the three quarts that are provided. For sorbets, you can frequently get away with just tossing in a can of fruit; however, for ice creams and gelatos, it's crucial that the ingredients include a mixture of fat and sugar to get the correct texture and consistency (including the juices).

Ninja advises freezing your components for at least 24 hours (the entire base needs to be between 9°F and -7°F); nevertheless, I've tried spinning my ingredients after only 18 hours and had decent luck. I guess it really depends on how cold your freezer is; if you had a blast chiller, I guess you could get away with a lot less waiting.

It's crucial to keep in mind that if your freezer is set to a very low temperature, you can wind up with the result that appears crumbly. Ninja advises that, in this case, you should just process the mixture once again using the re-spin feature. Personally, I find it simple to simply give a crumbly mixture a toss with my ice cream scoop and leave it to see it all come together. Your ingredients should be completely frozen before attaching the pint to the machine and choosing a program. The process of "creamifying" is when a very strong blade rotates and moves from the top to the bottom of the pint.

 **Main Functions of Ninja Creami**

The 5-in-1, 7-in-1, and 11-in-1 Deluxe versions of the Ninja CREAMi are available. I have the 7-in-1 model, which has preset programs for making milkshakes, ice cream, lite ice cream, sorbet, mix-ins, smoothie bowls, and gelato; the 11-in-1 Ninja CREAMi Deluxe has five new, exclusive Ninja CREAMi Deluxe features, including frozen drink, slushi, frozen yogurt, creamiccino, and Italian ice. The Smoothie Bowl feature is absent from the Deluxe version, but it features larger containers that hold more ice cream. The smoothie bowl and milkshake options are not available in the 5-in-1 option. The 5-in-1 option may be hard to find right now because it seems to have been discontinued. Three pint-sized containers, the machine itself, and a recipe book with 30 recipes are all included with the 7-in-1 Ninja CREAMi. The Ninja Creami has the following amazing functions:

## Scoopable Programs

·Ice Cream                              ·Lite Ice Cream
·Sorbet                                 ·Gelato (Not Available On All Models)

## Drinkable Programs

·Milkshake                              ·Mix-In

The outer bowl can be used to transport the CREAMi Pint once it has been taken out of the freezer. Each attachment is BPA-free and dishwasher-safe (top rack only). Make sure that the paddle, pint, outer bowl, and lids are all separated before placing the goods in the dishwasher. Remove all packaging from the unit. In warm, soapy water, clean the paddle, containers, and lids. Use a dishwashing tool with a handle to clean the paddle. Rinse everything thoroughly, then let it all air dry. Clean the control panel with a soft cloth.

### Using the Control Panel

Pressing the Power button will turn the gadget on or off. The install light will turn on if the gadget is fully constructed but not yet ready for use. If the light is blinking, make sure the bowl is placed properly. If the light is solid, make sure the paddle is in position.

### Progress Bar

The progress bar displays the status of the One-Touch program. All four progress bar LEDs will blink twice after the program is done churning off.

### Programs with One Touch

Each One-Touch program is skillfully designed to provide delicious meals in 1-2 and a half minutes. Programs vary in time and speed depending on the perfect conditions to produce wonderfully creamy results for a particular type of recipe.

## Scoopable Programs

### Ice-Cream
Designed for traditional sumptuous foods. Excellent for making dairy and dairy substitute recipes into thick, creamy, and scoopable ice cream.

### Lite Ice-Cream
This feature is made for those who are health-conscious to make ice cream that contains sugar substitutes, low-fat ingredients, or both. Choose between the keto and paleo diets when preparing recipes.

### Gelato
It is a custard-based ingredient for Italian ice cream (not available on all models). When given a choice, pick GELATO to create decadent, rich sweets.

### Sorbet
It is created to transform fruit-based recipes that are heavy on sugar and water into creamy pleasures.

## Drinkable Programs

### Milkshake
It is designed to swiftly and thickly brew milkshakes. Simply combine the milk, add-ins, and ice cream of your choice (either handmade or purchased) before selecting the Milkshake option.

### Mix-In
It is made to incorporate bits of candy, cookies, nuts, cereal, or frozen fruit to create a treat that has just been made or that was purchased at a store. It's preferable to add mix-ins in the midst of a CREAMi Pint. Use a spoon to make a hole that is 1 1/2 inches in diameter and reaches the bottom of the pint after processing it. Fill the pint hole with chopped or broken mix-ins, then run the MIX-IN software once again.

### Re-Spin
It is made to make sure that the texture is smooth after using one of the preset programs. When the base is extremely cold (below -7°F), and the consistency is crumbly rather than creamy, RE-SPIN is frequently required. Re-spinning is not recommended prior to utilizing the MIX-IN software. Press the program button that is lit to end an active program.

## Using Ninja Creami Ice Cream Maker

Before you first use the appliance, make sure the pint is clean and fixed in its place. Plug in the Ninja Creami and switch it on to get started. Fill the CREAMi Pint with the ingredients. Past the pint's MAX FILL line, do not add ingredients. On ninjacreami.com, you may pick from hundreds of recipes to discover the ingredients. Want to skip the 24-hour wait? Add mix-ins to store-bought ice cream to make it your own, or create a milkshake. If you want to personalize store-bought ice cream, scoop it into a pint and re-spin.

The device is not a blender, so do not process an ice block or ice cubes that are solid. Do not blend or process frozen fruit or other hard, brittle components. Fruit must either be mixed with other ingredients or frozen before processing in order to preserve its juice. If the recipe calls for frozen ingredients, put the pint's lid on and freeze it for at least a day. Plug in the unit and place it on a clean, dry, level surface such as a countertop or table.

### Freezing Tips

Make sure your freezer's temperature is set properly if it is programmable. The unit is made to handle bases that range in temperature from 9°F to -7°F. Your pint should get to the right temperature if your freezer is within this range.

Put the base in the freezer for at least a day. Although frozen, the base must first reach a lower temperature before processing. Do not freeze the pint at an angle in order to protect your appliance. Place the pint in the freezer on a flat surface. The best freezers are upright ones. Since chest freezers frequently get quite cold, I do not advise using them. Before assembly, the item must be connected to power. If the outer bowl is inserted before the unit is plugged in, the appliance will not operate.

Remove the pint lid and put the pint in the outer bowl once the base has been prepared or frozen. If ingredients have been frozen at an angle or if the pint has been scooped out and then re-frozen unevenly, do not process the pint to prevent damage to the machine.

## Smooth

Before re-freezing processed food in the pint, always smooth the surface. Put the pint in the refrigerator to enable the ingredients to thaw if the freezing is uneven. The components should then be well mixed by whisking. Place the pint on a level surface in the freezer and re-freeze. Insert the Creamerizer Paddle into the bottom of the outer bowl lid after depressing and holding the paddle latch on top of the lid. To lock the paddle, release the clasp. The paddle will be somewhat loose, and the latch will be in the middle when everything is entirely attached.

To ensure that the lines on the lid and handle are parallel, place the tab of the lid just slightly to the right of the outer bowl handle. To lock, turn the lid clockwise. Ensure that the device is plugged in. The outer bowl should then be set atop the motor base, with the handle positioned directly beneath the control panel. To elevate the platform and secure the bowl, turn the handle to the right. The bowl will click into place when it is fully inserted.

## Install

Turn the device on by pressing the power button. The One-Touch Program will flash, and the device will be ready for use if the outer bowl is inserted correctly. Choose the program that will serve your recipe the best. When finished, the software will shut off automatically. If the install light is on, the device is not ready for usage yet. Verify the bowl is inserted correctly if the light is blinking. Make sure the paddle is placed if the light is solid. Before inserting the bowl, be careful to plug the device in.

## Program for the Ninja Creami Ice Cream Maker

When the program is finished, twist the handle back to the center while holding the bowl release button on the left-hand side of the motor base. This will allow you to remove the outer bowl. The bowl will be lowered from the platform when the handle is turned. To remove, lift the bowl. Press the lid to unlock button, then turn the lid counterclockwise to remove it. Do not handle leftovers using the RE-SPIN software. The device does not support running One-Touch Programs back-to-back. After analyzing the results, continue after lowering the bowl between each program.

### Ice cream making with mix-ins

If adding mix-ins, use a spoon to make a hole that is 1 1/2 inches broad and reaches the pint's bottom. Repeat the previous mixing steps to process again using the MIX-IN option after adding chopped or broken mix-ins to the pint's hole.

## Add-On Tips

Add ¼ cup of your preferred crushed candies, frozen fruit, chopped nuts, chocolate chunks, and other ingredients. I advise not using more than ¼ cup of mix-ins when combining multiple different kinds. You are welcome to change the mix-ins' proportions to suit your preferences, but make sure the outer bowl's cover can still comfortably fit over the pint.

### Hard mix-ins will not break down.

Nuts, chocolate, and other mix-ins won't be broken down as part of the MIX-IN program. I advise using pre-chopped ingredients, micro chocolate chips, and candies.

**Soft additives will degrade.**

After the MIX-IN program, mix-ins, including cereal, cookies, and frozen fruit, will become smaller. I advise cutting soft items into larger pieces. I do not advise using fresh fruit, sauces, or spreads as mix-ins for ice cream or gelato. Your treat will become diluted if you add fresh fruit, fudge, or caramel sauce. Nut butter and chocolate hazelnut spread don't mix well, either. The use of frozen fruit or chocolate/caramel shell toppings is advised.

**Re-Spin**

RE-SPIN can be applied to a crumbly or powdery pint to make it more creamy if mix-ins aren't being added. Often, RE-SPIN is required for extremely cold bases. Repeat to process the base once more using the RE-SPIN software if it is crumbly or powdery. Re-spinning is not recommended prior to utilizing the MIX-IN software.

**How to Remove the Pint When Processing is done?**

Lift the pint out of the outer bowl. Rinse the outer bowl cover to get rid of any fragments stuck in the Creamerizer Paddle or sticky residue. Press the latch on the top of the outer bowl cover to release the paddle. Release the paddle into the sink for quick cleanup. By hitting the power button, you can turn the device off. When finished, unplug the device. For cleaning and storing instructions, see the Care & Maintenance section.

Have you finished your pint? Before freezing it again, use a spoon or spatula to flatten the top of your frozen dessert. Reprocess the treat using the same program you used to produce it if it becomes hard after being re-frozen. If it's soft, simply scoop some up and eat it.

Additional containers may be used to keep leftovers. However, to ensure that it may be processed once more if necessary, I advise keeping leftovers in a pint. If your treat includes mix-ins, processing it once more will probably crush the add-ins and provide a new flavor.

Rinse the outer bowl lid, then press the paddle clasp to release the Creamerizer paddle from the lid before cleaning.

### Hand-Washing

In warm, soapy water, wash the paddle lids and containers. To clean the paddle, use a dishwashing tool with a handle. All pieces should be thoroughly rinsed and air-dried.

### Dishwasher

Dishwasher-safe items include the paddle and containers (top rack only). Before putting them in the dishwasher, make sure the paddle, pint, outer bowl, and lids are all separated. To get the best results, wash any stuck-on ingredients in the dishwasher. Before cleaning the outer bowl cover, take out the paddle because it can have ingredients caught under it. Run warm water through the drain holes on either side of the paddle release lever after that. To completely drain the lid, position it so that the lever side is downward. Take off the center of the dark grey rubber lip seal that is attached to the underside of the outer bowl lid. After that, either run a dishwasher or hand-wash the lid and seal it in warm, soapy water.

## Cleaning

Before cleaning the motor base, unplug it. Use a clean, wet cloth to clean the motor base. To clean the base, avoid using abrasive rags, pads, or brushes. After each use, wipe the spindle beneath the control panel with a moist cloth. Raise the platform to clean if the liquid is caught between the motor base and the platform. The handle of the Outer Bowl should be positioned in the center below the control panel and on the motor base. To elevate the platform, turn the handle to the right. The space between the base and the raised platform should then be cleaned using a moist cloth.

## Storing

Near the rear of the motor base, wrap the cable with the hook-and-loop fastener for cold storage. Do not wrap the cord around the base's storage area's bottom. Do keep any extra attachments next to the

device or in a cabinet so they won't be lost or hurt or pose a safety risk.

**How to Recover from Auto-Shut-Off?**

If you accidentally overload this device, a special safety system protects the motor and drive system from damage. The motor will momentarily shut off if the device is overwhelmed. If this happens, follow this reset process.

·Disconnect the device from the outlet.

·Give the appliance around 15 minutes to cool.

·Take off the paddle and outer bowl lid. Make sure nothing is clogging the lid assembly.

Be careful not to go over the allowed capacities. The most frequent reason for appliance overload is this. Do not process an ice block or ice cubes that are solid. Make sure not to blend or process frozen fruit or other hard, brittle components. Fruit must either be mixed with other ingredients or frozen before processing in order to preserve its juice.

Troubleshooting

If you ever come across any problem while using this machine, then before troubleshooting, first turn off the power and unplug the equipment to lower the risk of shock and unintentional action. Let me help you deal with any of the following problems:

**While processing, my Ninja Cream Unit moves on the counter. What should I do?**

Make sure the countertop and the feet of the unit are clean and dry.

**My frozen treat is liquid, not solid, after processing. How to manage that?**

If a base is still soft after processing, re-freeze the CREAMi Pint for several hours or until the required consistency is achieved. For the best results, freeze the base for at least 24 hours before processing it right away after removing it. Try setting your freezer to a cooler temperature if the processed base is still not hard. The device is made to process bases in the 9°F to -7°F temperature range.

It's possible that your recipe has an excessive

amount of fat or sugar. For optimum results, refer to the inspiration manual and use the provided recipes as a general reference. When bases are frozen in extremely cold freezers, they may come out crumbly after processing; frozen sweets appear powdered or crumbly. Use the RE-SPIN program to smooth and cream your frozen delight after running a One-Touch program.

Your recipe can have too little sugar or fat. For optimum results, refer to the inspiration manual and use the provided recipes as a general reference.

**My One-Touch program won't light up. What should I do?**

Before inserting the outer bowl, be that the appliance is hooked into a functional outlet. Then choose a program by pressing the power button. Verify that the device is completely ready for use. The install light will blink if the outer bowl is incorrectly mounted while the appliance is powered on. The install light will turn on if the paddle is not installed properly. When the device is properly installed, all One-Touch Programs will be illuminated.

Running two programs simultaneously is not possible with this device. Lower the bowl between each program, evaluate the results, then raise the bowl to begin the next.

**The Installation light keeps blinking; why is that so?**

The outside bowl is either absent or improperly attached. Make sure the paddle is inserted into the outer bowl lid, and the outer bowl is covered. The outer bowl should then be placed onto the motor base with the handle positioned in the center beneath the control panel. To elevate the platform and secure the bowl, turn the handle to the right.

Install light is lighted consistently. The paddle is either missing or has been placed improperly, but the outer bowl is correctly in place. By depressing and holding the bowl release button to the left of the motor base and turning the outer bowl handle inward, you can lower the platform. Make certain the paddle is secured inside the lid.

One progress bar light, as well as all program lights, are flashing. What seems to be the problem?
The motor needs to be reset because it is overloaded. Remove the bowl, unplug the appliance, and let the motor base cool for about 15 minutes before turning it back on. Take off the paddle and lid of the outer bowl. Make sure nothing is clogging the lid assembly. It's possible that the substances you're processing are too dense. Make sure you use products that contain fat or sugar. For optimum results, adhere to the inspiration guide's recipes.

It could be really cold in your freezer. The device is made to process bases in the 9°F to -7°F temperature range. Alter the setting on your freezer, slide the pint to the front, or wait a few minutes before processing it out on the counter. Never prepare frozen fruit that is in a solid block, ice cubes, or hard, loose ingredients.

**The progress bar's middle two parts are blinking. Why?**
The program was unable to finish because of an error. After making sure the paddle is placed correctly, try running the software once more.

**My pint froze in the freezer at an angle. How to avoid that?**
Do not process a pint that has been frozen at an angle in order to protect the device. If the pint has been unevenly frozen after being scooped out, do not process it.

Before re-freezing, always smooth the ice cream's surface. Put the pint in the refrigerator to enable the ingredients to thaw if the freezing is uneven. The components should then be well mixed by whisking. Place the pint on a level surface in your freezer and re-freeze. After processing, the outer bowl won't come loose from the motor base. After about two minutes, try to remove the outer bowl once more. To remove the bowl handle, turn it clockwise while holding the release button on the left side of the motor base. That might require considerable force.

Prior to processing, make sure the chamber on top of the paddle is completely dry to avoid the outer bowl being caught on the motor base. Additionally, when processing successive bases, remember to rinse and dry the paddle after each base. Drying the paddle between runs will stop this from happening because, with some recipes, water may freeze between the paddle and motor base, causing them to cling together.

**My Ninja CREAMi Pint has scratches inside. How to avoid them?**

After frequent usage, little scratching of the pint is typical. Prepare ingredients in a separate bowl and refrain from using rough metal tools inside the pint to prevent scratches. Use soft, non-abrasive cloths to clean.

## Chapter 1 Milkshakes

# Vanilla Peanut Butter Milkshake

**Ingredients:**

1½ cups vanilla ice cream
½ cup unsweetened almond milk

¼ cup peanut butter
¼ teaspoon vanilla extract

**Preparation:**

1. In an empty Ninja CREAMi pint container, place the ice cream. 2. Top with the remaining ingredients and gently stir to combine. 3. Arrange the container into the outer bowl of Ninja CREAMi. 4. Install the "Creamerizer Paddle" onto the lid of outer bowl. 5. Then rotate the lid clockwise to lock. 6. Press "Power" button to turn on the unit. 7. Then press "MILKSHAKE" button. 8. When the program is completed, turn the outer bowl and release it from the machine. 9. Transfer the shake into serving glasses and enjoy immediately.

Nutritional Information per Serving: Calories: 304 | Fat: 22.4g | Sat Fat: 6.9g | Carbohydrates: 18.9g | Fiber: 2.6g | Sugar: 13.6g | Protein: 10g

# Lime Rainbow Sherbet Milkshake

**Ingredients:**

1½ cups rainbow sherbet

½ cup lime seltzer

**Preparation:**

1. In an empty Ninja CREAMi pint container, place sherbet and top with lime seltzer. 2. Arrange the container into the outer bowl of Ninja CREAMi. 3. Install the "Creamerizer Paddle" onto the lid of outer bowl. 4. Then rotate the lid clockwise to lock. 5. Press "Power" button to turn on the unit. 6. Then press "MILKSHAKE" button. 7. When the program is completed, turn the outer bowl and release it from the machine. 8. Transfer the shake into a serving glass and enjoy immediately.

Nutritional Information per Serving: Calories: 195 | Fat: 2.3g | Sat Fat: 1.5g | Carbohydrates: 40.5g | Fiber: 0g | Sugar: 30g | Protein: 1.5g

# Sugar Cookie Vanilla Milkshake

## Ingredients:

1 cup vanilla ice cream

1 cup oat milk

2 small sugar cookies, crushed

4 tablespoons sprinkles

## Preparation:

1. In an empty Ninja CREAMi pint container, place the ice cream. 2. With a spoon, create a 1½-inch wide hole in the center that reaches the bottom of the pint container. 3. Add the remaining ingredients into the hole. 4. Arrange the container into the outer bowl of Ninja CREAMi. 5. Install the "Creamerizer Paddle" onto the lid of outer bowl. 6. Then rotate the lid clockwise to lock. 7. Press "Power" button to turn on the unit. 8. Then press "MILKSHAKE" button. 9. When the program is completed, turn the outer bowl and release it from the machine. 10. Transfer the shake into serving glasses and enjoy immediately.

**Nutritional Information per Serving:** Calories: 212 | Fat: 8.3g | Sat Fat: 4.3g | Carbohydrates: 34.2g | Fiber: 5.1g | Sugar: 23g | Protein: 4.3g

# Tasty Amaretto Cookies Milkshake

Preparation Time: 10 minutes | Servings: 2

## Ingredients:

1 cup whole milk

½ cup amaretto-flavored coffee creamer

¼ cup amaretto liqueur

1 tablespoon agave nectar

¼ cup chocolate chip cookies, chopped

## Preparation:

1. In an empty Ninja CREAMi pint container, place milk and remaining ingredients except for cookies and stir to combine. 2. Cover the container with the storage lid and freeze for 24 hours. 3. After 24 hours, remove the lid from container and arrange into the outer bowl of Ninja CREAMi. 4. Install the "Creamerizer Paddle" onto the lid of outer bowl. 5. Then rotate the lid clockwise to lock. 6. Press "Power" button to turn on the unit. 7. Then press "MILKSHAKE" button. 8. When the program is completed, turn the outer bowl and release it from the machine. 9. Transfer the shake into serving glasses and sprinkle with chopped chocolate chip cookies, enjoy immediately.

**Nutritional Information per Serving:** Calories: 371 | Fat: 17.6g | Sat Fat: 9.5g | Carbohydrates: 25.9g | Fiber: 1g | Sugar: 42.2g | Protein: 6.5g

# Vanilla Almond Milkshake

Preparation Time: 10 minutes | Servings: 2

## Ingredients:

1½ cups vanilla ice cream
½ cup unsweetened almond milk
2 tablespoons honey

¼ cup almonds, chopped
½ teaspoon ground cinnamon
¼ teaspoon vanilla extract

## Preparation:

1. In an empty Ninja CREAMi pint container, place ice cream, followed by almond milk, honey, almonds, cinnamon and vanilla extract. 2. Arrange the container into the outer bowl of Ninja CREAMi. 3. Install the "Creamerizer Paddle" onto the lid of outer bowl. 4. Then rotate the lid clockwise to lock. 5. Press "Power" button to turn on the unit. 6. Then press "MILKSHAKE" button. 7. When the program is completed, turn the outer bowl and release it from the machine. 8. Transfer the shake into serving glasses and enjoy immediately.

**Nutritional Information per Serving:** Calories: 248 | Fat: 12.1g | Sat Fat: 3.9g | Carbohydrates: 32.9g | Fiber: 2.5g | Sugar: 28.3g | Protein: 4.6g

# Coconut Avocado Milkshake

Preparation Time: 10 minutes | Servings: 2

## Ingredients:

1 cup coconut ice cream
1 small ripe avocado, peeled, pitted and chopped
1 teaspoon fresh lemon juice
2 tablespoons agave nectar

1 teaspoon vanilla extract
Pinch of salt
½ cup oat milk

## Preparation:

1. In an empty Ninja CREAMi pint container, place ice cream, followed by remaining ingredients. 2. Arrange the container into the outer bowl of Ninja CREAMi. 3. Install the "Creamerizer Paddle" onto the lid of outer bowl. 4. Then rotate the lid clockwise to lock. 5. Press "Power" button to turn on the unit. 6. Then press "MILKSHAKE" button. 7. When the program is completed, turn the outer bowl and release it from the machine. 8. Transfer the shake into serving glasses and enjoy immediately.

**Nutritional Information per Serving:** Calories: 373 | Fat: 23.7g | Sat Fat: 6.4g | Carbohydrates: 39g | Fiber: 8.5g | Sugar: 27.6g | Protein: 4.1g

# Strawberry Oreo Milkshake

## Ingredients:

1½ cups strawberry ice cream
¼ cup mini Oreo cookies

¼ cup milk

## Preparation:

1. In an empty Ninja CREAMi pint container, place the ice cream. 2. With a spoon, create a 1½-inch wide hole in the center that reaches the bottom of the pint container. 3. Add the cookies into the hole and top with milk. 4. Arrange the container into the outer bowl of Ninja CREAMi. 5. Install the "Creamerizer Paddle" onto the lid of outer bowl. 6. Then rotate the lid clockwise to lock. 7. Press "Power" button to turn on the unit. 8. Then press "MILKSHAKE" button. 9. When the program is completed, turn the outer bowl and release it from the machine. 10. Transfer the shake into a serving glass and enjoy immediately.

**Nutritional Information per Serving:** Calories: 346 | Fat: 16g | Sat Fat: 9.2g | Carbohydrates: 43.7g | Fiber: 1.7g | Sugar: 32.3g | Protein: 6.9g

# Easy Chocolate Milkshake

## Ingredients:

1½ cups chocolate ice cream
½ cup unsweetened chocolate almond milk

## Preparation:

1. In an empty Ninja CREAMi pint container, place ice cream, followed by almond milk. 2. Arrange the container into the outer bowl of Ninja CREAMi. 3. Install the "Creamerizer Paddle" onto the lid of outer bowl. 4. Then rotate the lid clockwise to lock. 5. Press "Power" button to turn on the unit. 6. Then press "MILKSHAKE" button. 7. When the program is completed, turn the outer bowl and release it from the machine. 8. Transfer the shake into serving glasses and enjoy immediately.

**Nutritional Information per Serving:** Calories: 113 | Fat: 6.1g | Sat Fat: 3.5g | Carbohydrates: 12.5g | Fiber: 0.6g | Sugar: 10.5g | Protein: 2g

# Coffee Vodka Vanilla Milkshake

**Ingredients:**

2 cups vanilla ice cream
2 tablespoons coffee liqueur

2 tablespoons vodka

**Preparation:**

1. In an empty Ninja CREAMi pint container, place ice cream, followed by coffee liqueur and vodka. 2. Arrange the container into the outer bowl of Ninja CREAMi. 3. Install the "Creamerizer Paddle" onto the lid of outer bowl. 4. Then rotate the lid clockwise to lock. 5. Press "Power" button to turn on the unit. 6. Then press "MILKSHAKE" button. 7. When the program is completed, turn the outer bowl and release it from the machine. 8. Transfer the shake into serving glasses and enjoy immediately.

**Nutritional Information per Serving:** Calories: 226 | Fat: 7.1g | Sat Fat: 4.5g | Carbohydrates: 24.1g | Fiber: 0.5g | Sugar: 22.1g | Protein: 2.3g

# Chocolate Liqueur Vanilla Milkshake

Preparation Time: 10 minutes | Servings: 2

**Ingredients:**

2 cups vanilla ice cream
⅓ cup chocolate liqueur

⅓ cup whole milk

**Preparation:**

1. In an empty Ninja CREAMi pint container, place ice cream, followed by chocolate liqueur and milk. 2. Arrange the container into the outer bowl of Ninja CREAMi. 3. Install the "Creamerizer Paddle" onto the lid of outer bowl. 4. Then rotate the lid clockwise to lock. 5. Press "Power" button to turn on the unit. 6. Then press "MILKSHAKE" button. 7. When the program is completed, turn the outer bowl and release it from the machine. 8. Transfer the shake into serving glasses and enjoy immediately.

**Nutritional Information per Serving:** Calories: 313 | Fat: 8.5g | Sat Fat: 5.3g | Carbohydrates: 39.6g | Fiber: 0.5g | Sugar: 37.7g | Protein: 3.7g

# Ginger Chocolate Milkshake

## Ingredients:

1½ cups chocolate ice cream
½ cup oat milk

1 teaspoon ground ginger
¼ cup chocolate, grated

## Preparation:

1. In an empty Ninja CREAMi pint container, place the ice cream. 2. With a spoon, create a 1½-inch wide hole in the center that reaches the bottom of the pint container. 3. Add the remaining ingredients into the hole. 4. Arrange the container into the outer bowl of Ninja CREAMi. 5. Install the "Creamerizer Paddle" onto the lid of outer bowl. 6. Then rotate the lid clockwise to lock. 7. Press "Power" button to turn on the unit. 8. Then press "MILKSHAKE" button. 9. When the program is completed, turn the outer bowl and release it from the machine. 10. Transfer the shake into serving glasses and enjoy immediately.

Nutritional Information per Serving: Calories: 251 | Fat: 12.2g | Sat Fat: 7.8g | Carbohydrates: 31.1g | Fiber: 1.7g | Sugar: 26.1g | Protein: 4.4g

# Homemade Vanilla Ice Cream Milkshake

## Ingredients:

2 cups vanilla ice cream
1 cup whole milk

1 teaspoon vanilla extract

## Preparation:

1. In an empty Ninja CREAMi pint container, place the ice cream. 2. Top with the milk and vanilla extract and gently stir to combine. 3. Arrange the container into the outer bowl of Ninja CREAMi. 4. Install the "Creamerizer Paddle" onto the lid of outer bowl. 5. Then rotate the lid clockwise to lock. 6. Press "Power" button to turn on the unit. 7. Then press "MILKSHAKE" button. 8. When the program is completed, turn the outer bowl and release it from the machine. 9. Transfer the shake into serving glasses and enjoy immediately.

Nutritional Information per Serving: Calories: 216 | Fat: 11g | Sat Fat: 6.8g | Carbohydrates: 21.8g | Fiber: 0.5g | Sugar: 20.7g | Protein: 6.2g

# Oreo Vanilla Milkshake

Preparation Time: 10 minutes | Servings: 2

## Ingredients:

2 cups vanilla ice cream
⅔ cup milk

8 Oreo cookies, crushed
1 teaspoon vanilla extract

## Preparation:

1. In an empty Ninja CREAMi pint container, place the ice cream. 2. Top with the remaining ingredients and gently stir to combine. 3. Arrange the container into the outer bowl of Ninja CREAMi. 4. Install the "Creamerizer Paddle" onto the lid of outer bowl. 5. Then rotate the lid clockwise to lock. 6. Press "Power" button to turn on the unit. 7. Then press "MILKSHAKE" button. 8. When the program is completed, turn the outer bowl and release it from the machine. 9. Transfer the shake into serving glasses and enjoy immediately.

Nutritional Information per Serving: Calories: 370 | Fat: 16.3g | Sat Fat: 7g | Carbohydrates: 48.9g | Fiber: 1.7g | Sugar: 34.2g | Protein: 7.1g

# Chocolate Cookie n' Cream Milkshake

Preparation Time: 10 minutes | Servings: 2

## Ingredients:

1½ cups cookie n' cream ice cream
½ cup whole milk

2 tablespoons cream cheese, softened
3 chocolate sandwich cookies, crushed

## Preparation:

1. In an empty Ninja CREAMi pint container, place the ice cream. 2. Top with the remaining ingredients and gently stir to combine. 3. Arrange the container into the outer bowl of Ninja CREAMi. 4. Install the "Creamerizer Paddle" onto the lid of outer bowl. 5. Then rotate the lid clockwise to lock. 6. Press "Power" button to turn on the unit. 7. Then press "MILKSHAKE" button. 8. When the program is completed, turn the outer bowl and release it from the machine. 9. Transfer the shake into serving glasses and enjoy immediately.

Nutritional Information per Serving: Calories: 339 | Fat: 18.2g | Sat Fat: 8.2g | Carbohydrates: 42g | Fiber: 0.4g | Sugar: 13.7g | Protein: 6g

# Coffee Ice Cream Milkshake

## Ingredients:

1½ cups coffee ice cream
½ cup whole milk

## Preparation:

1. In an empty Ninja CREAMi pint container, place the ice cream, followed by milk. 2. Arrange the container into the outer bowl of Ninja CREAMi. 3. Install the "Creamerizer Paddle" onto the lid of outer bowl. 4. Then rotate the lid clockwise to lock. 5. Press "Power" button to turn on the unit. 6. Then press "MILKSHAKE" button. 7. When the program is completed, turn the outer bowl and release it from the machine. 8. Transfer the shake into serving glasses and enjoy immediately.

**Nutritional Information per Serving:** Calories: 142 | Fat: 7.2g | Sat Fat: 4.5g | Carbohydrates: 14g | Fiber: 0g | Sugar: 14.5g | Protein: 4.2g

# Yummy Banana Milkshake

## Ingredients:

1 scoop vanilla ice cream
2 small bananas, peeled and halved

7 fluid ounces semi-skimmed milk

## Preparation:

1. In an empty Ninja CREAMi pint container, place the ice cream. 2. Top with the remaining ingredients and gently stir to combine. 3. Arrange the container into the outer bowl of Ninja CREAMi. 4. Install the "Creamerizer Paddle" onto the lid of outer bowl. 5. Then rotate the lid clockwise to lock. 6. Press "Power" button to turn on the unit. 7. Then press "MILKSHAKE" button. 8. When the program is completed, turn the outer bowl and release it from the machine. 9. Transfer the shake into serving glasses and enjoy immediately.

**Nutritional Information per Serving:** Calories: 210 | Fat: 4.9g | Sat Fat: 2.4g | Carbohydrates: 36.3g | Fiber: 2.8g | Sugar: 19,4g | Protein: 5.4g

# Fresh Strawberry Milkshake

## Ingredients:

1½ ounces vanilla ice cream

5¼ ounces fresh strawberries, hulled and halved

3 ounces whole milk

## Preparation:

1. In an empty Ninja CREAMi pint container, place the ice cream. 2. Top with the strawberries and milk and gently stir to combine. 3. Arrange the container into the outer bowl of Ninja CREAMi. 4. Install the "Creamerizer Paddle" onto the lid of outer bowl. 5. Then rotate the lid clockwise to lock. 6. Press "Power" button to turn on the unit. 7. Then press "MILKSHAKE" button. 8. When the program is completed, turn the outer bowl and release it from the machine. 9. Transfer the shake into serving glasses and enjoy immediately.

**Nutritional Information per Serving:** Calories: 152 | Fat: 6.9g | Sat Fat: 4.2g | Carbohydrates: 19.6g | Fiber: 1.9g | Sugar: 16.4g | Protein: 3.6g

# Delicious Coconut Chai Tea Milkshake

## Ingredients:

½ cup coconut milk

2 chai tea bags

1½ cups vanilla coconut milk ice cream

## Preparation:

1. Place a small pot on the stove over medium heat, add the coconut milk, bring to a simmer, and then remove from the heat. 2. Steep the chai tea bags in the coconut milk until it reaches room temperature. 3. Squeeze the tea bags into the coconut milk once it has cooled. 4. Fill an empty CREAMi Pint with the ice cream. 5. Create a 1-inch wide hole in the bottom of the pint using a spoon. Fill the hole with the remaining ingredients. 6. Place the pint into the outer bowl of the Ninja CREAMi. 7. Install the Creamerizer Paddle onto the lid of the outer bowl, then rotate the lid clockwise to lock. 8. Turn the unit on. 9. Press the MILKSHAKE button. 10. When the program is complete, turn the outer bowl and release it from the machine. 11. Transfer the shake into serving glasses and serve immediately.

**Nutritional Information per Serving:** Calories: 241 | Fat: 19g | Sat Fat: 16g | Carbohydrates: 15g | Fiber: 1g | Sugar: 12g | Protein: 3g

# Vanilla Peach Milkshake

## Ingredients:

1½ cups vanilla ice cream

¼ cup peach, peeled, pitted and sliced

½ cup unsweetened vanilla almond milk

## Preparation:

1. In an empty Ninja CREAMi pint container, place the ice cream. 2. Top with the peach slices and milk and gently stir to combine. 3. Arrange the container into the outer bowl of Ninja CREAMi. 4. Install the "Creamerizer Paddle" onto the lid of outer bowl. 5. Then rotate the lid clockwise to lock. 6. Press "Power" button to turn on the unit. 7. Then press "MILKSHAKE" button. 8. When the program is completed, turn the outer bowl and release it from the machine. 9. Transfer the shake into serving glasses and enjoy immediately.

**Nutritional Information per Serving:** Calories: 120 | Fat: 6.2g | Sat Fat: 3.5g | Carbohydrates: 14.3g | Fiber: 0.9g | Sugar: 12.3g | Protein: 2.2g

# Coconut Cacao Milkshake

## Ingredients:

1½ cups vanilla coconut ice cream

½ cup canned full fat coconut milk

1 teaspoon matcha powder

¼ cup cacao nibs

1 teaspoon peppermint extract

## Preparation:

1. Fill an empty CREAMi Pint with the ice cream. 2. Create a 1-inch wide hole in the bottom of the pint using a spoon. Fill the hole with the remaining ingredients. 3. Place the pint into the outer bowl of the Ninja CREAMi. 4. Install the Creamerizer Paddle onto the lid of the outer bowl, then rotate the lid clockwise to lock. 5. Turn on the unit. 6. Press the MILKSHAKE button. 7. When the program is complete, turn the outer bowl and release it from the machine. 8. Transfer the shake into serving glasses and serve immediately.

**Nutritional Information per Serving:** Calories: 237 | Fat: 17g | Sat Fat: 14g | Carbohydrates: 16g | Fiber: 2.4g | Sugar: 12g | Protein: 2g

# Strawberry Marshmallow Milkshake

**Ingredients:**

1½ cups strawberry ice cream
½ cup milk

1 tablespoon marshmallow topping

**Preparation:**

1. Fill an empty CREAMi Pint with the ice cream. 2. Create a 1-inch wide hole in the bottom of the pint using a spoon. Fill the hole with the remaining ingredients. 3. Place the pint into the outer bowl of the Ninja CREAMi. 4. Install the Creamerizer Paddle onto the lid of the outer bowl, then rotate the lid clockwise to lock. 5. Turn the unit on. 6. Press the MILKSHAKE button. 7. When the program is complete, turn the outer bowl and release it from the machine. 8. Transfer the shake into serving glasses and serve immediately.

**Nutritional Information per Serving:** Calories: 135 | Fat: 6g | Sat Fat: 4g | Carbohydrates: 13g | Fiber: 0g | Sugar: 12g | Protein: 3g

# Mocha Tahini Milkshake

Preparation Time: 10 minutes | Servings: 2

**Ingredients:**

1½ cups chocolate ice cream
½ cup unsweetened oat milk
¼ cup tahini

2 tablespoons coffee
1 tablespoon chocolate fudge

**Preparation:**

1. In an empty Ninja CREAMi pint container, place ice cream followed by milk, tahini, coffee and fudge. 2. Arrange the container into the Outer Bowl of Ninja CREAMi. 3. Install the Creamerizer Paddle onto the lid of Outer Bowl. 4. Then rotate the lid clockwise to lock. 5. Press Power button to turn on the unit. 6. Then press Milkshake button. 7. When the program is completed, turn the Outer Bowl and release it from the machine. 8. Transfer the shake into serving glasses and serve immediately.

**Nutritional Information per Serving:** Calories: 174 | Fat: 11.4g | Sat Fat: 3g | Carbohydrates: 15.2g | Fiber: 2g | Sugar: 9.5g | Protein: 4.1g

# Strawberry Shortcake Milkshake

## Ingredients:

1½ cups strawberry ice cream
½ cup whole milk

¼ premade pound cake, crumbled
¼ cup fresh strawberries, trimmed, cut in quarters

## Preparation:

1. Fill an empty CREAMi Pint with the ice cream. 2. Create a 1-inch wide hole in the bottom of the pint using a spoon. Fill the hole with the remaining ingredients. 3. Arrange the container into the outer bowl of the Ninja CREAMi. 4. Install the Creamerizer Paddle onto the lid of the outer bowl, then rotate the lid clockwise to lock. 5. Turn the unit on. 6. Press the MILKSHAKE button. 7. When the program is complete, turn the outer bowl and release it from the machine. 8. Transfer the shake into serving glasses and serve immediately.

**Nutritional Information per Serving:** Calories: 347 | Fat: 14g | Sat Fat: 4g | Carbohydrates: 34g | Fiber: 0.9g | Sugar: 13g | Protein: 5g

# Healthy Blueberry Ice Cream Milkshake

## Ingredients:

2¼ cups blueberry ice cream
¾ cup whole milk

## Preparation:

1. In an empty Ninja CREAMi pint container, place ice cream, followed by milk. 2. Arrange the container into the outer bowl of Ninja CREAMi. 3. Install the "Creamerizer Paddle" onto the lid of outer bowl. 4. Then rotate the lid clockwise to lock. 5. Press "Power" button to turn on the unit. 6. Then press "MILKSHAKE" button. 7. When the program is completed, turn the outer bowl and release it from the machine. 8. Transfer the shake into serving glasses and enjoy immediately.

**Nutritional Information per Serving:** Calories: 209 | Fat: 10.9g | Sat Fat: 6.8g | Carbohydrates: 22.1g | Fiber: 0.6g | Sugar: 20.6g | Protein: 5.5g

# Chapter 2 Smoothie Bowls

# Banana Coconut Rum Smoothie

## Ingredients:

½ of ripe banana, peeled and cut in ½-inch pieces
¼ cup coconut rum
¼ cup coconut cream

½ cup unsweetened canned coconut milk
¾ cup pineapple juice
2 tablespoons fresh lime juice

## Preparation:

1. In a large-sized bowl, add banana and remaining ingredients and whisk until blended thoroughly. 2. Transfer the blended mixture into an empty Ninja CREAMi pint container. 3. Cover the container with a storage lid and freeze for 24 hours. 4. After 24 hours, remove the lid from the container and arrange it into the outer bowl of Ninja CREAMi. 5. Install the "Creamerizer Paddle" onto the lid of the outer bowl. 6. Then rotate the lid clockwise to lock. 7. Press "Power" button to turn on the unit. 8. Then press "SMOOTHIE BOWL" button. 9. When the program is completed, turn the outer bowl and release it from the machine. 10. Transfer the smoothie into serving bowls and enjoy immediately.

Nutritional Information per Serving: Calories: 301 | Fat: 15.6g | Sat Fat: 13.9g | Carbohydrates: 22.1g | Fiber: 1.6g | Sugar: 15.5g | Protein: 2.1g

# Papaya Orange Smoothie Bowl

## Ingredients:

1 cup frozen papaya chunks
1 cup plain Greek yogurt
¼ cup fresh orange juice

2 tablespoons maple syrup
½ teaspoon ground cinnamon

## Preparation:

1. In a high-powered blender, add papaya and remaining ingredients and process until smooth. 2. Transfer the blended mixture into an empty Ninja CREAMi pint container. 3. Cover the container with storage lid and freeze for 24 hours. 4. After 24 hours, remove the lid from container and arrange into the outer bowl of Ninja CREAMi. 5. Install the "Creamerizer Paddle" onto the lid of outer bowl. 6. Then rotate the lid clockwise to lock. 7. Press "Power" button to turn on the unit. 8. Then press "SMOOTHIE BOWL" button. 9. When the program is completed, turn the outer bowl and release it from the machine. 10. Transfer the smoothie into serving bowls and enjoy immediately.

Nutritional Information per Serving: Calories: 186 | Fat: 1.8g | Sat Fat: 1.3g | Carbohydrates: 33.6g | Fiber: 1.6g | Sugar: 28.8g | Protein: 7.6g

# Delicious Mango Smoothie Bowl

Preparation Time: 10 minutes | Servings: 2

## Ingredients:

2 cups ripe mango, peeled and cut into 1-inch pieces
14 ounces coconut milk

2-3 drops liquid stevia
¼ teaspoon vanilla extract

## Preparation:

1. Place the mango pieces into an empty Ninja CREAMi pint container. 2. Top with coconut milk, stevia and vanilla extract and stir to combine. 3. Cover the container with the storage lid and freeze for 24 hours. 4. After 24 hours, remove the lid from container and arrange into the outer bowl of Ninja CREAMi. 5. Install the "Creamerizer Paddle" onto the lid of outer bowl. 6. Then rotate the lid clockwise to lock. 7. Press "Power" button to turn on the unit. 8. Then press "SMOOTHIE BOWL" button. 9. When the program is completed, turn the outer bowl and release it from the machine. 10. Transfer the smoothie into serving bowls and enjoy immediately.

Nutritional Information per Serving: Calories: 220 | Fat: 7.1g | Sat Fat: 3.9g | Carbohydrates: 33.8g | Fiber: 2.6g | Sugar: 33.1g | Protein: 7.7g

# Peach & Grapefruit Smoothie Bowl

Preparation Time: 10 minutes | Servings: 2

## Ingredients:

1 cup frozen peach pieces
1 cup vanilla Greek yogurt
¼ cup fresh grapefruit juice

2 tablespoons honey
¼ teaspoon vanilla extract
½ teaspoon ground cinnamon

## Preparation:

1. In a high-powered blender, add peach pieces and remaining ingredients and process until smooth. 2. Transfer the blended mixture into an empty Ninja CREAMi pint container. 3. Cover the container with storage lid and freeze for 24 hours. 4. After 24 hours, remove the lid from container and arrange into the outer bowl of Ninja CREAMi. 5. Install the "Creamerizer Paddle" onto the lid of outer bowl. 6. Then rotate the lid clockwise to lock. 7. Press "Power" button to turn on the unit. 8. Then press "SMOOTHIE BOWL" button. 9. When the program is completed, turn the outer bowl and release it from the machine. 10. Transfer the smoothie into serving bowls and enjoy immediately.

Nutritional Information per Serving: Calories: 197 | Fat: 1.8g | Sat Fat: 1.2g | Carbohydrates: 36.7g | Fiber: 1.6g | Sugar: 35.6g | Protein: 8g

# Fresh Melon & Pineapple Smoothie Bowl

**Ingredients:**

3½ ounces melon chunks
3½ ounces pineapple chunks

5¼ ounces vanilla yogurt
3½ fluid ounces whole milk

**Preparation:**

1. Place the melon and pineapple chunks into an empty Ninja CREAMi pint container and stir to combine. 2. Top with yogurt and milk. 3. Cover the container with storage lid and freeze for 24 hours. 4. After 24 hours, remove the lid from container and arrange into the outer bowl of Ninja CREAMi. 5. Install the "Creamerizer Paddle" onto the lid of outer bowl. 6. Then rotate the lid clockwise to lock. 7. Press "Power" button to turn on the unit. 8. Then press "SMOOTHIE BOWL" button. 9. When the program is completed, turn the outer bowl and release it from the machine. 10. Transfer the smoothie into serving bowls and enjoy immediately.

**Nutritional Information per Serving:** Calories: 334 | Fat: 8.1g | Sat Fat: 4.8g | Carbohydrates: 46.5g | Fiber: 6.1g | Sugar: 28.9g | Protein: 27.2g

# Honey Raspberry & Orange Smoothie Bowl

**Ingredients:**

2 cups fresh raspberries
½ cup vanilla yogurt

¼ cup fresh orange juice
1 tablespoon honey

**Preparation:**

1. In an empty Ninja CREAMi pint container, place the raspberries and with the back of a spoon, firmly press the berries below the MAX FILL line. 2. Add the yogurt, orange juice and honey and stir to combine. 3. Cover the container with storage lid and freeze for 24 hours. 4. After 24 hours, remove the lid from container and arrange into the outer bowl of Ninja CREAMi. 5. Install the "Creamerizer Paddle" onto the lid of outer bowl. 6. Then rotate the lid clockwise to lock. 7. Press "Power" button to turn on the unit. 8. Then press "SMOOTHIE BOWL" button. 9. When the program is completed, turn the outer bowl and release it from the machine. 10. Transfer the smoothie into serving bowls and enjoy immediately.

**Nutritional Information per Serving:** Calories: 152 | Fat: 3.1g | Sat Fat: 1.5g | Carbohydrates: 29.8g | Fiber: 8.1g | Sugar: 19.9g | Protein: 4g

# Blueberry-Banana Smoothie Bowl

## Ingredients:

1 frozen banana
¾ cup frozen blueberries
1 tablespoon peanut butter

½ tablespoon pure maple syrup
1 scoop vanilla protein powder
½ cup unsweetened almond milk

## Preparation:

1. In a large-sized high-powered blender, add banana and remaining the ingredients and process until smooth. 2. Transfer the blended mixture into an empty Ninja CREAMi pint container. 3. Cover the container with storage lid and freeze for 24 hours. 4. After 24 hours, remove the lid from container and arrange into the outer bowl of Ninja CREAMi. 5. Install the "Creamerizer Paddle" onto the lid of outer bowl. 6. Then rotate the lid clockwise to lock. 7. Press "Power" button to turn on the unit. 8. Then press "SMOOTHIE BOWL" button. 9. When the program is completed, turn the outer bowl and release it from the machine. 10. Transfer the smoothie into serving bowls and enjoy immediately.

**Nutritional Information per Serving:** Calories: 212 | Fat: 6.2g | Sat Fat: 1.5g | Carbohydrates: 28.6g | Fiber: 3.6g | Sugar: 16.8g | Protein: 14g

# Mixed Berries Chia Smoothie Bowl

## Ingredients:

1 cup full-fat coconut milk
1 tablespoon chia seeds
1 banana, peeled

1 cup mixed berries
2 scoops whey protein powder

## Preparation:

1. In a large-sized high-powered blender, add coconut milk and remaining ingredients and process until smooth. 2. Transfer the blended mixture into an empty Ninja CREAMi pint container. 3. Cover the container with storage lid and freeze for 24 hours. 4. After 24 hours, remove the lid from container and arrange into the outer bowl of Ninja CREAMi. 5. Install the "Creamerizer Paddle" onto the lid of outer bowl. 6. Then rotate the lid clockwise to lock. 7. Press "Power" button to turn on the unit. 8. Then press "SMOOTHIE BOWL" button. 9. When the program is completed, turn the outer bowl and release it from the machine. 10. Transfer the smoothie into serving bowls and enjoy immediately.

**Nutritional Information per Serving:** Calories: 278 | Fat: 9g | Sat Fat: 6.6g | Carbohydrates: 27.6g | Fiber: 5.3g | Sugar: 13.1g | Protein: 23.8g

# Frozen Fruit & Banana Smoothie Bowl

## Ingredients:

1 ripe banana, peeled and cut in 1-inch pieces

2 cups frozen fruit mix

1¼ cups vanilla yogurt

## Preparation:

1. In a large-sized high-powered blender, add banana, fruit mix and yogurt and process until smooth. 2. Transfer the blended mixture into an empty Ninja CREAMi pint container. 3. Cover the container with storage lid and freeze for 24 hours. 4. After 24 hours, remove the lid from container and arrange into the outer bowl of Ninja CREAMi. 5. Install the "Creamerizer Paddle" onto the lid of outer bowl. 6. Then rotate the lid clockwise to lock. 7. Press "Power" button to turn on the unit. 8. Then press "SMOOTHIE BOWL" button. 9. When the program is completed, turn the outer bowl and release it from the machine. 10. Transfer the smoothie into serving bowls and enjoy immediately.

**Nutritional Information per Serving:** Calories: 221 | Fat: 2.1g | Sat Fat: 1.6g | Carbohydrates: 40.3g | Fiber: 4.5g | Sugar: 30g | Protein: 9.4g

# Coconut Banana Smoothie Bowl

## Ingredients:

½ of ripe banana, peeled and cut in ½-inch pieces

¼ cup coconut rum

¼ cup unsweetened coconut cream

½ cup unsweetened canned coconut milk

¾ cup pineapple juice

2 tablespoons fresh lime juice

## Preparation:

1. In a large-sized bowl, add banana and remaining ingredients and whisk until blended thoroughly. 2. Transfer the blended mixture into an empty Ninja CREAMi pint container. 3. Cover the container with storage lid and freeze for 24 hours. 4. After 24 hours, remove the lid from container and arrange into the outer bowl of Ninja CREAMi. 5. Install the "Creamerizer Paddle" onto the lid of outer bowl. 6. Then rotate the lid clockwise to lock. 7. Press "Power" button to turn on the unit. 8. Then press "SMOOTHIE BOWL" button. 9. When the program is completed, turn the outer bowl and release it from the machine. 10. Transfer the smoothie into serving bowls and enjoy immediately.

**Nutritional Information per Serving:** Calories: 309 | Fat: 17.1g | Sat Fat: 14.9g | Carbohydrates: 23.5g | Fiber: 2.3g | Sugar: 15g | Protein: 2.3

# Blueberry-Banana Smoothie Bowl

## Ingredients:

1 cup frozen blueberries
1 fresh banana, peeled and halved
⅛ teaspoon lemon zest

½ teaspoon vanilla extract
2 tablespoons almond milk

## Preparation:

1. In a high-powered blender, add blueberries and remaining ingredients and process until smooth. 2. Transfer the blended mixture into an empty Ninja CREAMi pint container. 3. Cover the container with storage lid and freeze for 24 hours. 4. After 24 hours, remove the lid from container and arrange into the outer bowl of Ninja CREAMi. 5. Install the "Creamerizer Paddle" onto the lid of outer bowl. 6. Then rotate the lid clockwise to lock. 7. Press "Power" button to turn on the unit. 8. Then press "SMOOTHIE BOWL" button. 9. When the program is completed, turn the outer bowl and release it from the machine. 10. Transfer the smoothie into serving bowls and enjoy immediately.

**Nutritional Information per Serving:** Calories: 105 | Fat: 0.8g | Sat Fat: 0.3g | Carbohydrates: 24.9g | Fiber: 3.3g | Sugar: 15.3g | Protein: 1.7g

# Fresh Strawberry & Banana Smoothie Bowl

## Ingredients:

4 ounces fresh strawberries, hulled and thinly sliced
2¾ ounces ripe bananas, peeled and thinly sliced

5¼ ounces plain yogurt
3½ fluid ounces whole milk

## Preparation:

1. In an empty Ninja CREAMi pint container, place the fruit slices. 2. Top with yogurt and milk. 3. Cover the container with storage lid and freeze for 24 hours. 4. After 24 hours, remove the lid from container and arrange into the outer bowl of Ninja CREAMi. 5. Install the "Creamerizer Paddle" onto the lid of outer bowl. 6. Then rotate the lid clockwise to lock. 7. Press "Power" button to turn on the unit. 8. Then press "SMOOTHIE BOWL" button. 9. When the program is completed, turn the outer bowl and release it from the machine. 10. Transfer the smoothie into serving bowls and enjoy immediately.

**Nutritional Information per Serving:** Calories: 138 | Fat: 2.9g | Sat Fat: 1.8g | Carbohydrates: 20.9g | Fiber: 2.1g | Sugar: 15.6g | Protein: 6.8g

# Cranberry & Cherry Smoothie Bowl

## Ingredients:

1½ cups frozen cranberries
½ cup frozen cherries
1 cup apple juice

⅓ cup agave nectar
½ teaspoon cinnamon

## Preparation:

1. In an empty Ninja CREAMi pint container, place cranberries and cherries. 2. In a large-sized bowl, add the apple juice, agave nectar and cinnamon and whisk until blended thoroughly. 3. Place the blended mixture over the fruit and gently stir to blend. 4. Cover the container with storage lid and freeze for 24 hours. 5. After 24 hours, remove the lid from container and arrange into the outer bowl of Ninja CREAMi. 6. Install the "Creamerizer Paddle" onto the lid of outer bowl. 7. Then rotate the lid clockwise to lock. 8. Press "Power" button to turn on the unit. 9. Then press "SMOOTHIE BOWL" button. 10. When the program is completed, turn the outer bowl and release it from the machine. 11. Transfer the smoothie into serving bowls and enjoy immediately.

**Nutritional Information per Serving:** Calories: 281 | Fat: 0.3g | Sat Fat: 0.1g | Carbohydrates: 68.9g | Fiber: 6.9g | Sugar: 58.5g | Protein: 0.5g

# Delicious Pineapple & Mango Smoothie Bowl

## Ingredients:

½ cup hemp milk
¾ cup full-fat coconut milk
1 cup pineapple chunks
¾ cup mango chunks

1 teaspoon vanilla extract
1 tablespoon chia seeds
1 scoop active whey protein powder

## Preparation:

1. In a large-sized high-powered blender, add hemp milk and remaining ingredients and process until smooth. 2. Transfer the blended mixture into an empty Ninja CREAMi pint container. 3. Cover the container with storage lid and freeze for 24 hours. 4. After 24 hours, remove the lid from container and arrange into the outer bowl of Ninja CREAMi. 5. Install the "Creamerizer Paddle" onto the lid of outer bowl. 6. Then rotate the lid clockwise to lock. 7. Press "Power" button to turn on the unit. 8. Then press "SMOOTHIE BOWL" button. 9. When the program is completed, turn the outer bowl and release it from the machine. 10. Transfer the smoothie into serving bowls and enjoy immediately.

**Nutritional Information per Serving:** Calories: 364 | Fat: 22.2g | Sat Fat: 17.3g | Carbohydrates: 28.4g | Fiber: 3.6g | Sugar: 20.3g | Protein: 15.2g

# Dragon Fruit & Strawberries Yogurt Smoothie Bowl

## Ingredients:

1 cup frozen dragon fruit pieces
1½ cups fresh strawberries, hulled and quartered
½ cup plain yogurt

2 tablespoons agave nectar
1 tablespoon fresh lime juice

## Preparation:

1. In a high-powered blender, add fruit pieces and remaining ingredients and process until smooth. 2. Transfer the blended mixture into an empty Ninja CREAMi pint container. 3. Cover the container with storage lid and freeze for 24 hours. 4. After 24 hours, remove the lid from container and arrange into the outer bowl of Ninja CREAMi. 5. Install the "Creamerizer Paddle" onto the lid of outer bowl. 6. Then rotate the lid clockwise to lock. 7. Press "Power" button to turn on the unit. 8. Then press "SMOOTHIE BOWL" button. 9. When the program is completed, turn the outer bowl and release it from the machine. 10. Transfer the smoothie into serving bowls and enjoy immediately.

Nutritional Information per Serving: Calories: 162 | Fat: 1.1g | Sat Fat: 0.6g | Carbohydrates: 34.8g | Fiber: 3.2g | Sugar: 30.6g | Protein: 4.2g

# Tasty Mixed Fruit Smoothie Bowl

## Ingredients:

½ cup water
1 cup frozen pineapple, chopped
1 cup frozen mango, chopped
1 cup frozen dragon fruit, chopped

1 cup frozen strawberries, hulled
1 banana, peeled
1-2 tablespoons honey

## Preparation:

1. In a high-powered blender, add water and remaining ingredients and process until smooth. 2. Transfer the blended mixture into an empty Ninja CREAMi pint container. 3. Cover the container with storage lid and freeze for 24 hours. 4. After 24 hours, remove the lid from container and arrange into the outer bowl of Ninja CREAMi. 5. Install the "Creamerizer Paddle" onto the lid of outer bowl. 6. Then rotate the lid clockwise to lock. 7. Press "Power" button to turn on the unit. 8. Then press "SMOOTHIE BOWL" button. 9. When the program is completed, turn the outer bowl and release it from the machine. 10. Transfer the smoothie into serving bowls and enjoy immediately.

Nutritional Information per Serving: Calories: 222 | Fat: 0.6g | Sat Fat: 0.2g | Carbohydrates: 57.8g | Fiber: 5.5g | Sugar: 45.7g | Protein: 1.8g

# Chocolate Banana Chia Smoothie Bowl

## Ingredients:

1 cup full-fat coconut milk

2 tablespoon cacao powder

1 tablespoon chia seeds

1½ bananas, peeled and sliced

1½ scoops protein powder

## Preparation:

1. In a high-powered blender, add water and remaining ingredients and process until smooth. 2. Transfer the blended mixture into an empty Ninja CREAMi pint container. 3. Cover the container with storage lid and freeze for 24 hours. 4. After 24 hours, remove the lid from container and arrange into the outer bowl of Ninja CREAMi. 5. Install the "Creamerizer Paddle" onto the lid of outer bowl. 6. Then rotate the lid clockwise to lock. 7. Press "Power" button to turn on the unit. 8. Then press "SMOOTHIE BOWL" button. 9. When the program is completed, turn the outer bowl and release it from the machine. 10. Transfer the smoothie into serving bowls and enjoy immediately.

**Nutritional Information per Serving:** Calories: 433 | Fat: 27.9g | Sat Fat: 23.5g | Carbohydrates: 30.9g | Fiber: 5.1g | Sugar: 13.5g | Protein: 20.8g

# Avocado, Kale & Green Apple Smoothie Bowl

## Ingredients:

1 banana, peeled and cut into 1-inch pieces

½ of avocado, peeled, pitted and cut into 1-inch pieces

1 cup fresh kale leaves

1 cup green apple, peeled, cored and cut into 1-inch pieces

¼ cup unsweetened coconut milk

2 tablespoons agave nectar

## Preparation:

1. In a large high-speed blender, add all the ingredients and pulse until smooth. 2. Transfer the mixture into an empty Ninja CREAMi pint container. 3. Cover the container with storage lid and freeze for 24 hours. 4. After 24 hours, remove the lid from container and arrange into the Outer Bowl of Ninja CREAMi. 5. Install the Creamerizer Paddle onto the lid of Outer Bowl. 6. Then rotate the lid clockwise to lock. 7. Press Power button to turn on the unit. 8. Then press Smoothie Bowl button. 9. When the program is completed, turn the Outer Bowl and release it from the machine. 10. Transfer the smoothie into serving bowls and serve immediately.

**Nutritional Information per Serving:** Calories: 179 | Fat: 8.7g | Sat Fat: 4.2g | Carbohydrates: 27.2g | Fiber: 4.9g | Sugar: 17.5g | Protein: 1.8g

# Banana Oats Smoothie Bowl

## Ingredients:

½ cup water
¼ cup quick oats
1 cup vanilla Greek yogurt

½ cup banana, peeled and sliced
3 tablespoons honey

## Preparation:

1. In a small microwave-safe bowl, add the water and oats and microwave on High or about one minute. 2. Remove from the microwave and stir in the yogurt, banana and honey until well combined. 3. Transfer the mixture into an empty Ninja CREAMi pint container. 4. Cover the container with storage lid and freeze for 24 hours. 5. After 24 hours, remove the lid from container and arrange into the Outer Bowl of Ninja CREAMi. 6. Install the Creamerizer Paddle onto the lid of Outer Bowl. 7. Then rotate the lid clockwise to lock. 8. Press Power button to turn on the unit. 9. Then press Smoothie Bowl button. 10. When the program is completed, turn the Outer Bowl and release it from the machine. 11. Transfer the smoothie into serving bowls and serve with your favorite topping.

**Nutritional Information per Serving:** Calories: 278 | Fat: 2.7g | Sat Fat: 1.1g | Carbohydrates: 55.7g | Fiber: 2.1g | Sugar: 41.6g | Protein: 10.9g

# Pitaya Pineapple Smoothie Bowl

## Ingredients:

2 cups frozen pitaya chunks
1 can pineapple juice

## Preparation:

1. Mix the pitaya chunks and pineapple juice until well combined in a large bowl. 2. Transfer the mixture into an empty Ninja CREAMi Pint. 3. Cover the pint with the lid and freeze for 24 hours. 4. After 24 hours, remove the lid from the pint and place it into the outer bowl of the Ninja CREAMi. 5. Install the Creamerizer Paddle onto the lid of the outer bowl, then rotate the lid clockwise to lock. 6. Turn the unit on. 7. Press the SMOOTHIE BOWL button. 8. When the program is complete, turn the outer bowl and release it from the machine. 9. Transfer the smoothie into serving bowls and serve with your favorite toppings.

**Nutritional Information per Serving:** Calories: 45 | Fat: 0g | Sat Fat: 0g | Carbohydrates: 11g | Fiber: 1g | Sugar: 9g | Protein: 0.5g

# Gingered Mango Orange Smoothie Bowl

## Ingredients:

1 cup frozen mango, cubed
1 cup plain whole milk
¼ cup orange juice

2 tablespoons maple syrup
½ teaspoon ground ginger
Pinch black pepper

## Preparation:

1. Mix all the ingredients until well combined in a large bowl. 2. Transfer the mixture into an empty Ninja CREAMi Pint. 3. Cover the pint with the lid and freeze for 24 hours. 4. After 24 hours, remove the lid and place the pint into the outer bowl of the Ninja CREAMi. 5. Install the Creamerizer Paddle onto the lid of the outer bowl, then rotate the lid clockwise to lock. 6. Turn the unit on. 7. Press the SMOOTHIE BOWL button. 8. When the program is complete, turn the outer bowl and release it from the machine. 9. Transfer the smoothie into serving bowls and serve with your favorite toppings.

**Nutritional Information per Serving:** Calories: 90 | Fat: 2.2g | Sat Fat: 1g | Carbohydrates: 15g | Fiber: 0.7g | Sugar: 15g | Protein: 2g

# Mixed Berries Smoothie Bowl

## Ingredients:

1 cup fresh blueberries
1 cup fresh blackberries
1 cup fresh raspberries

¼ cup yogurt
1 tablespoon honey

## Preparation:

1. Mix all the ingredients until well combined in a large bowl. 2. Transfer the mixture into an empty Ninja CREAMi Pint. 3. Cover the pint with the lid and freeze for 24 hours. 4. After 24 hours, remove the lid and place the pint into the outer bowl of the Ninja CREAMi. 5. Install the Creamerizer Paddle onto the lid of the outer bowl, then rotate the lid clockwise to lock. 6. Turn the unit on. 7. Press the SMOOTHIE BOWL button. 8. When the program is complete, turn the outer bowl and release it from the machine. 9. Transfer the smoothie into serving bowls and serve with your favorite toppings.

**Nutritional Information per Serving:** Calories: 79 | Fat: 0.7g | Sat Fat: 0.2g | Carbohydrates: 16g | Fiber: 4g | Sugar: 12g | Protein: 2g

# Avocado-Banana Smoothie Bowl

**Ingredients:**

½ cup unsweetened coconut milk
¼ cup fresh apple juice
2 tablespoons whey protein isolate
4-5 tablespoons maple syrup

¼ teaspoon vanilla extract
1 cup ripe avocado, peeled, pitted and cut in ½-inch pieces
1 cup fresh banana, peeled and cut in ½-inch pieces

**Preparation:**

1. In a large-sized bowl, add the coconut milk, apple juice, protein isolate, maple syrup and vanilla extract and whisk until blended thoroughly. 2. Place the avocado and banana into an empty Ninja CREAMi pint container and with the back of a spoon, firmly press the fruit below the MAX FILL line. 3. Top with coconut milk mixture and mix until blended thoroughly. 4. Cover the container with storage lid and freeze for 24 hours. 5. After 24 hours, remove the lid from container and arrange into the outer bowl of Ninja CREAMi. 6. Install the "Creamerizer Paddle" onto the lid of outer bowl. 7. Then rotate the lid clockwise to lock. 8. Press "Power" button to turn on the unit. 9. Then press "SMOOTHIE BOWL" button. 10. When the program is completed, turn the outer bowl and release it from the machine. 11. Transfer the smoothie into serving bowls and enjoy immediately.

Nutritional Information per Serving: Calories: 252 | Fat: 14.6g | Sat Fat: 7.9g | Carbohydrates: 28.9g | Fiber: 4.1g | Sugar: 19.2g | Protein: 4.9g

# Creamy Banana Peanut Butter Smoothie Bowl

## Ingredients:

2 frozen ripe bananas, peeled
2 tablespoons creamy peanut butter
2 tablespoons flaxseed meal

½ teaspoon vanilla extract
¼ cup unsweetened almond milk

## Preparation:

1. In a high-powered blender, add bananas and remaining ingredients and process until smooth. 2. Transfer the blended mixture into an empty Ninja CREAMi pint container. 3. Cover the container with storage lid and freeze for 24 hours. 4. After 24 hours, remove the lid from container and arrange into the outer bowl of Ninja CREAMi. 5. Install the "Creamerizer Paddle" onto the lid of outer bowl. 6. Then rotate the lid clockwise to lock. 7. Press "Power" button to turn on the unit. 8. Then press "SMOOTHIE BOWL" button. 9. When the program is completed, turn the outer bowl and release it from the machine. 10. Transfer the smoothie into serving bowls and enjoy immediately.

**Nutritional Information per Serving:** Calories: 244 | Fat: 11.1g | Sat Fat: 2.2g | Carbohydrates: 32.5g | Fiber: 6.1g | Sugar: 16.2g | Protein: 6.7g

# Chapter 3 Ice Creams

# Delicious Cherry Ice Cream

Preparation Time: 10 minutes | Servings: 4

## Ingredients:

1 cup full-fat coconut milk
1¼ cups frozen cherries

1 teaspoon almond extract

## Preparation:

1. 1n a high-powered blender, add coconut milk and remaining ingredients and process until smooth. 2. Transfer the blended mixture into an empty Ninja CREAMi pint container. 3. Cover the container with storage lid and freeze for 24 hours. 4. After 24 hours, remove the lid from container and arrange into the outer bowl of Ninja CREAMi. 5. Install the "Creamerizer Paddle" onto the lid of outer bowl. 6. Then rotate the lid clockwise to lock. 7. Press "Power" button to turn on the unit. 8. Then press "ICE CREAM" button. 9. When the program is completed, turn the outer bowl and release it from the machine. 10. Transfer the ice cream into serving bowls and enjoy immediately.

**Nutritional Information per Serving:** Calories: 145 | Fat: 12.2g | Sat Fat: 11.1g | Carbohydrates: 7.5g | Fiber: 0.8g | Sugar: 5.5g | Protein: 1.5g

# Maple Peanut Butter Ice Cream

Preparation Time: 10 minutes | Servings: 4

## Ingredients:

1 cup whole milk
¾ cup heavy cream
2 tablespoons peanut butter

½ banana, peeled
1 teaspoon vanilla extract
¼ cup maple syrup

## Preparation:

1. 1n a high-powered blender, add milk and remaining ingredients and process until smooth. 2. Transfer the blended mixture into an empty Ninja CREAMi pint container. 3. Cover the container with storage lid and freeze for 24 hours. 4. After 24 hours, remove the lid from container and arrange into the outer bowl of Ninja CREAMi. 5. Install the "Creamerizer Paddle" onto the lid of outer bowl. 6. Then rotate the lid clockwise to lock. 7. Press "Power" button to turn on the unit. 8. Then press "ICE CREAM" button. 9. When the program is completed, turn the outer bowl and release it from the machine. 10. Transfer the ice cream into serving bowls and enjoy immediately.

**Nutritional Information per Serving:** Calories: 229 | Fat: 14.4g | Sat Fat: 7.2g | Carbohydrates: 21.7g | Fiber: 0.9g | Sugar: 17.6g | Protein: 4.6g

# Homemade Vanilla Ice Cream

## Ingredients:

½ tablespoon cream cheese, softened
⅓ cup sugar
1 teaspoon vanilla bean paste

1¼ cups milk
½ cup heavy whipping cream

## Preparation:

1. In a large-sized bowl, add cream cheese, sugar, and vanilla bean paste and with a whisk, blend until blended thoroughly. 2. Add in the milk and heavy whipping cream and whisk until blended thoroughly. 3. Transfer the blended mixture into an empty Ninja CREAMi pint container. 4. Cover the container with storage lid and freeze for 24 hours. 5. After 24 hours, remove the lid from container and arrange into the outer bowl of Ninja CREAMi. 6. Install the "Creamerizer Paddle" onto the lid of outer bowl. 7. Then rotate the lid clockwise to lock. 8. Press the "Power" button to turn on the unit. 9. Then press "ICE CREAM" button. 10. When the program is completed, turn the outer bowl and release it from the machine. 11. Transfer the ice cream into serving bowls and enjoy immediately.

Nutritional Information per Serving: Calories: 162 | Fat: 7.6g | Sat Fat: 4.7g | Carbohydrates: 22.1g | Fiber: 0g | Sugar: 21.4g | Protein: 2.9g

# Cottage Cheese Vanilla Ice Cream

## Ingredients:

1 cup cottage cheese
1 cup unsweetened vanilla almond milk
2 tablespoons pure maple syrup

1 scoop vanilla protein powder
1 teaspoon ground cinnamon
Pinch of salt

## Preparation:

1. In a high-powered blender, add cottage cheese and remaining ingredients and process until smooth. 2. Transfer the blended mixture into an empty Ninja CREAMi pint container. 3. Cover the container with storage lid and freeze for 24 hours. 4. After 24 hours, remove the lid from container and arrange into the outer bowl of Ninja CREAMi. 5. Install the "Creamerizer Paddle" onto the lid of outer bowl. 6. Then rotate the lid clockwise to lock. 7. Press "Power" button to turn on the unit. 8. Then press "ICE CREAM" button. 9. When the program is completed, turn the outer bowl and release it from the machine. 10. Transfer the ice cream into serving bowls and enjoy immediately.

Nutritional Information per Serving: Calories: 104 | Fat: 2.4g | Sat Fat: 0.9g | Carbohydrates: 10.3g | Fiber: 0.6g | Sugar: 6.4g | Protein: 10.3g

# Vanilla Orange Ice Cream

## Ingredients:

¾ cup oat milk

½ cup coconut cream

¼ cup frozen orange juice concentrate

3½ tablespoons instant vanilla pudding mix

2 tablespoons sugar

1 teaspoon vanilla extract

## Preparation:

1. In a large-sized bowl, add oat milk and remaining ingredients and whisk until blended thoroughly. 2. Transfer the blended mixture into an empty Ninja CREAMi pint container. 3. Cover the container with storage lid and freeze for 24 hours. 4. After 24 hours, remove the lid from container and arrange into the outer bowl of Ninja CREAMi. 5. Install the "Creamerizer Paddle" onto the lid of outer bowl. 6. Then rotate the lid clockwise to lock. 7. Press "Power" button to turn on the unit. 8. Then press "ICE CREAM" button. 9. When the program is completed, turn the outer bowl and release it from the machine. 10. Transfer the ice cream into serving bowls and enjoy immediately.

**Nutritional Information per Serving:** Calories: 168 | Fat: 7.7g | Sat Fat: 6.4g | Carbohydrates: 24.3g | Fiber: 1.1g | Sugar: 21.1g | Protein: 1.6g

# Aromatic Apple Cider Ice Cream

## Ingredients:

1 cup heavy cream

½ cup whole milk

½ cup apple cider

1 teaspoon vanilla extract

⅓ cup light brown sugar

1 teaspoon ground cinnamon, divided

Pinch of ground allspice

Pinch of ground nutmeg

Pinch of ground cloves

2 teaspoons orange zest

## Preparation:

1. In a large-sized bowl, add heavy cream and remaining ingredients and whisk until blended thoroughly. 2. Transfer the blended mixture into an empty Ninja CREAMi pint container. 3. Cover the container with storage lid and freeze for 24 hours. 4. After 24 hours, remove the lid from container and arrange into the outer bowl of Ninja CREAMi. 5. Install the "Creamerizer Paddle" onto the lid of outer bowl. 6. Then rotate the lid clockwise to lock. 7. Press "Power" button to turn on the unit. 8. Then press "ICE CREAM" button. 9. When the program is completed, turn the outer bowl and release it from the machine. 10. Transfer the ice cream into serving bowls and enjoy immediately.

**Nutritional Information per Serving:** Calories: 188 | Fat: 12.2g | Sat Fat: 7.5g | Carbohydrates: 18.7g | Fiber: 0.5g | Sugar: 16.9g | Protein: 1.7g

# Banana Monk Fruit Ice Cream

## Ingredients:

1½ cups overripe bananas, peeled and sliced
3 tablespoons monk fruit sweetener

1 cup coconut cream
1 teaspoon banana extract

## Preparation:

1. In a bowl, add the coconut cream and whisk until smooth. 2. Add the banana slices and with the back of a fork, lightly mash them. 3. Add in the monk fruit sweetener and banana extract and stir until blended thoroughly. 4. Transfer the blended mixture into an empty Ninja CREAMi pint container. 5. Cover the container with storage lid and freeze for 24 hours. 6. After 24 hours, remove the lid from container and arrange into the outer bowl of Ninja CREAMi. 7. Install the "Creamerizer Paddle" onto the lid of outer bowl. 8. Then rotate the lid clockwise to lock. 9. Press "Power" button to turn on the unit. 10. Then press "ICE CREAM" button. 11. When the program is completed, turn the outer bowl and release it from the machine. 12. Transfer the ice cream into serving bowls and enjoy immediately.

Nutritional Information per Serving: Calories: 191 | Fat: 14.5g | Sat Fat: 12.7g | Carbohydrates: 16.3g | Fiber: 2.8g | Sugar: 9g | Protein: 2g

# Maple Sweet Potato Ice Cream

## Ingredients:

1¼ cups full-fat coconut milk
1 teaspoon vanilla extract
½ cup sweet potato puree

1½ teaspoons pumpkin pie spice
¼ cup maple syrup

## Preparation:

1. In a bowl, add coconut milk and remaining ingredients and whisk until blended thoroughly. 2. Transfer the blended mixture into an empty Ninja CREAMi pint container. 3. Cover the container with storage lid and freeze for 24 hours. 4. After 24 hours, remove the lid from container and arrange into the outer bowl of Ninja CREAMi. 5. Install the "Creamerizer Paddle" onto the lid of outer bowl. 6. Then rotate the lid clockwise to lock. 7. Press "Power" button to turn on the unit. 8. Then press "ICE CREAM" button. 9. When the program is completed, turn the outer bowl and release it from the machine. 10. Transfer the ice cream into serving bowls and enjoy immediately.

Nutritional Information per Serving: Calories: 229 | Fat: 15.2g | Sat Fat: 13.8g | Carbohydrates: 21.5g | Fiber: 0.9g | Sugar: 14.8g | Protein: 1.8g

# Pumpkin Ice Cream

## Ingredients:

1 tablespoon cream cheese
⅓ cup light brown sugar
1 teaspoon ground cinnamon
1 teaspoon vanilla extract

1 cup whole milk
¾ cup heavy cream
3 tablespoons pumpkin puree

## Preparation:

1. In a large-sized microwave-safe bowl, add the cream cheese and microwave on High for about 10 seconds. 2. Remove from the microwave and stir until smooth. 3. Add the brown sugar, cinnamon and vanilla extract and with a wire whisk, beat until the mixture looks like frosting. 4. Slowly add the milk, heavy cream and pumpkin puree and whisk until blended thoroughly. 5. Transfer the blended mixture into an empty Ninja CREAMi pint container. 6. Cover the container with storage lid and freeze for 24 hours. 7. After 24 hours, remove the lid from container and arrange into the outer bowl of Ninja CREAMi. 8. Install the "Creamerizer Paddle" onto the lid of outer bowl. 9. Then rotate the lid clockwise to lock. 10. Press "Power" button to turn on the unit. 11. Then press "ICE CREAM" button. 12. When the program is completed, turn the outer bowl and release it from the machine. 13. Transfer the ice cream into serving bowls and enjoy immediately.

**Nutritional Information per Serving:** Calories: 177 | Fat: 11.2g | Sat Fat: 6.9g | Carbohydrates: 16.8g | Fiber: 0.6g | Sugar: 15.5g | Protein: 2.8g

# Vanilla Banana Yogurt Ice Cream

## Ingredients:

1 cup plain yogurt
¼ cup maple syrup
1 tablespoon cream cheese, softened

1½ teaspoons vanilla extract
2 bananas, peeled and sliced

## Preparation:

1. In a large-sized bowl, add yogurt, maple syrup, cream cheese and vanilla extract and whisk until blended thoroughly. 2. Add the banana slices and stir to blend. 3. Transfer the blended mixture into an empty Ninja CREAMi pint container. 4. Cover the container with storage lid and freeze for 24 hours. 5. After 24 hours, remove the lid from container and arrange into the outer bowl of Ninja CREAMi. 6. Install the "Creamerizer Paddle" onto the lid of outer bowl. 7. Then rotate the lid clockwise to lock. 8. Press "Power" button to turn on the unit. 9. Then press "ICE CREAM" button. 10. When the program is completed, turn the outer bowl and release it from the machine. 11. Transfer the ice cream into serving bowls and enjoy immediately.

**Nutritional Information per Serving:** Calories: 161 | Fat: 1.9g | Sat Fat: 1.2g | Carbohydrates: 31.3g | Fiber: 1.5g | Sugar: 23.5g | Protein: 4.3g

# Homemade Raspberry Ice Cream

## Ingredients:

1 cup fresh raspberries, roughly chopped
¼ cup granulated sugar

1 cup whole milk
½ cup heavy whipping cream

## Preparation:

1. In a small-sized saucepan, add chopped raspberries and sugar and stir to blend. 2. Place the pan of raspberries over medium heat and cook for approximately 3-5 minutes, stirring occasionally. 3. Remove the pan of raspberries from heat and transfer in to a small-sized bowl. 4. Set aside to cool for a few minutes. 5. In the bowl of raspberries, add milk and heavy whipping cream and with an immersion blender, blend until smooth. 6. Transfer the blended mixture into an empty Ninja CREAMi pint container. 7. Cover the container with storage lid and freeze for 24 hours. 8. After 24 hours, remove the lid from container and arrange into the outer bowl of Ninja CREAMi. 9. Install the "Creamerizer Paddle" onto the lid of outer bowl. 10. Then rotate the lid clockwise to lock. 11. Press "Power" button to turn on the unit. 12. Then press "ICE CREAM" button. 13. When the program is completed, turn the outer bowl and release it from the machine. 14. Transfer the ice cream into serving bowls and enjoy immediately.

Nutritional Information per Serving: Calories: 151 | Fat: 7.7g | Sat Fat: 4.6g | Carbohydrates: 19.4g | Fiber: 2g | Sugar: 17.1g | Protein: 2.6g

# Pineapple Rum Ice Cream

## Ingredients:

8 ounces canned pineapple chunks in juice
½ cup lite coconut cream
¼ cup maple syrup

1½ teaspoons rum extract
½ cup banana, peeled and sliced

## Preparation:

1. In a large-sized bowl, add pineapple chunks, coconut cream, maple syrup and rum extract and stir until blended thoroughly. 2. Add banana slices and gently stir to blend. 3. Transfer the blended mixture into an empty Ninja CREAMi pint container. 4. Cover the container with storage lid and freeze for 24 hours. 5. After 24 hours, remove the lid from container and arrange into the outer bowl of Ninja CREAMi. 6. Install the "Creamerizer Paddle" onto the lid of outer bowl. 7. Then rotate the lid clockwise to lock. 8. Press "Power" button to turn on the unit. 9. Then press "ICE CREAM" button. 10. When the program is completed, turn the outer bowl and release it from the machine. 11. Transfer the ice cream into serving bowls and enjoy immediately.

Nutritional Information per Serving: Calories: 165 | Fat: 77.3g | Sat Fat: 6.4g | Carbohydrates: 26.6g | Fiber: 1.9g | Sugar: 20.6g | Protein: 1.2g

# Lime Watermelon Ice Cream

## Ingredients:

2 cups watermelon, peeled, seeded and cubed

2 tablespoons fresh lime juice

3 tablespoons agave nectar

## Preparation:

1. In an empty Ninja CREAMi pint container, place the watermelon cubes. 2. Top with the lime juice and agave nectar and gently stir to combine. 3. Arrange the container into the outer bowl of Ninja CREAMi. 4. Cover the container with storage lid and freeze for 24 hours. 5. After 24 hours, remove the lid from container and arrange into the outer bowl of Ninja CREAMi. 6. Install the "Creamerizer Paddle" onto the lid of outer bowl. 7. Then rotate the lid clockwise to lock. 8. Press "Power" button to turn on the unit. 9. Then press "ICE CREAM" button. 10. When the program is completed, turn the outer bowl and release it from the machine. 11. Transfer the ice cream into serving bowls and enjoy immediately.

**Nutritional Information per Serving:** Calories: 69 | Fat: 0.1g | Sat Fat: 0.1g | Carbohydrates: 17.8g | Fiber: 1.1g | Sugar: 15.9g | Protein: 0.5g

# Lime Avocado Ice Cream

## Ingredients:

1 (13½-ounce) can full-fat coconut milk

2 avocados, peeled and pitted

1 cup maple syrup

1 tablespoon lime zest

½ cup fresh lime juice

¼ cup water

## Preparation:

1. In a large-sized high-powered blender, add all of the ingredients and process until smooth. 2. Transfer the blended mixture into an empty Ninja CREAMi pint container. 3. Cover the container with storage lid and freeze for 24 hours. 4. After 24 hours, remove the lid from container and arrange into the outer bowl of Ninja CREAMi. 5. Install the "Creamerizer Paddle" onto the lid of outer bowl. 6. Then rotate the lid clockwise to lock. 7. Press "Power" button to turn on the unit. 8. Then press "ICE CREAM" button. 9. When the program is completed, turn the outer bowl and release it from the machine. 10. Transfer the ice cream into serving bowls and enjoy immediately.

**Nutritional Information per Serving:** Calories: 411 | Fat: 37.3g | Sat Fat: 20.3g | Carbohydrates: 18.9g | Fiber: 6.9g | Sugar: 2g | Protein: 3.4g

# Pumpkin Vanilla Ice Cream

## Ingredients:

1¼ cups full-fat coconut milk, warmed and cooled
½ cup canned pumpkin puree
½ cup brown sugar, packed
1 tablespoon rum

2 teaspoons pure vanilla paste
½ teaspoon ground cinnamon
¼ teaspoon ground nutmeg
⅛ teaspoon xanthan gum

## Preparation:

1. In a large-sized high-powered blender, add all of the ingredients and process until smooth. 2. Transfer the blended mixture into an empty Ninja CREAMi pint container. 3. Transfer the blended mixture into an empty Ninja CREAMi pint container. 4. Cover the container with storage lid and freeze for 24 hours. 5. After 24 hours, remove the lid from container and arrange into the outer bowl of Ninja CREAMi. 6. Install the "Creamerizer Paddle" onto the lid of outer bowl. 7. Then rotate the lid clockwise to lock. 8. Press "Power" button to turn on the unit. 9. Then press "ICE CREAM" button. 10. When the program is completed, turn the outer bowl and release it from the machine. 11. Transfer the ice cream into serving bowls and enjoy immediately.

**Nutritional Information per Serving:** Calories: 234 | Fat: 15.1g | Sat Fat: 13.8g | Carbohydrates: 23.3g | Fiber: 1.2g | Sugar: 19.9g | Protein: 1.6g

# Sea Salt Bourbon Caramel Ice Cream

## Ingredients:

1 (14-ounce) can dulce de leche
1¼ cups heavy cream

1 teaspoon sea salt flakes
1-3 tablespoons bourbon

## Preparation:

1. In a large-sized bowl, place dulce de leche, cream and salt and with a hand mixer, whisk until mixture becomes thick. 2. Add in the bourbon and gently stir to blend. 3. Transfer the blended mixture into an empty Ninja CREAMi pint container. 4. Cover the container with storage lid and freeze for 24 hours. 5. After 24 hours, remove the lid from container and arrange into the outer bowl of Ninja CREAMi. 6. Install the "Creamerizer Paddle" onto the lid of outer bowl. 7. Then rotate the lid clockwise to lock. 8. Press "Power" button to turn on the unit. 9. Then press "ICE CREAM" button. 10. When the program is completed, turn the outer bowl and release it from the machine. 11. Transfer the ice cream into serving bowls and enjoy immediately.

**Nutritional Information per Serving:** Calories: 435 | Fat: 27.1g | Sat Fat: 15.3g | Carbohydrates: 47.4g | Fiber: 0g | Sugar: 39.7g | Protein: 0.8g

# Chocolate Coconut Ice Cream

## Ingredients:

1 tablespoon cream cheese, softened

⅓ cup coconut sugar

1 teaspoon almond extract

2 tablespoons cocoa powder

1 cup coconut milk

¾ cup coconut cream

## Preparation:

1. In a large-sized microwave-safe bowl, add the cream cheese and microwave on High for about 10 seconds. 2. Remove from the microwave and stir until smooth. 3. Add the sugar, almond extract and cocoa powder with a wire whisk, whisk until the mixture looks like frosting. 4. Slowly add the coconut milk and coconut cream and whisk until blended thoroughly. 5. Transfer the blended mixture into an empty Ninja CREAMi pint container. 6. Cover the container with storage lid and freeze for 24 hours. 7. After 24 hours, remove the lid from container and arrange into the outer bowl of Ninja CREAMi. 8. Install the "Creamerizer Paddle" onto the lid of outer bowl. 9. Then rotate the lid clockwise to lock. 10. Press "Power" button to turn on the unit. 11. Then press "ICE CREAM" button. 12. When the program is completed, turn the outer bowl and release it from the machine. 13. Transfer the ice cream into serving bowls and enjoy immediately.

**Nutritional Information per Serving:** Calories: 319 | Fat: 26.3g | Sat Fat: 23g | Carbohydrates: 23.5g | Fiber: 3.1g | Sugar: 19.7g | Protein: 3.1g

# Classic Coffee Ice Cream

## Ingredients:

1 cup unsweetened almond milk

¾ cup heavy cream

3 tablespoons monk fruit sweetener

2 tablespoons raw agave nectar

1½ tablespoons instant coffee

1 teaspoon vanilla extract

## Preparation:

1. In a large-sized bowl, add almond milk and remaining ingredients and whisk until blended thoroughly. 2. Transfer the blended mixture into an empty Ninja CREAMi pint container. 3. Cover the container with storage lid and freeze for 24 hours. 4. After 24 hours, remove the lid from container and arrange into the outer bowl of Ninja CREAMi. 5. Install the "Creamerizer Paddle" onto the lid of outer bowl. 6. Then rotate the lid clockwise to lock. 7. Press "Power" button to turn on the unit. 8. Then press "ICE CREAM" button. 9. When the program is completed, turn the outer bowl and release it from the machine. 10. Transfer the ice cream into serving bowls and enjoy immediately.

**Nutritional Information per Serving:** Calories: 121 | Fat: 9.2g | Sat Fat: 5.3g | Carbohydrates: 9.3g | Fiber: 0.8g | Sugar: 7.7g | Protein: 0.7g

# Sweet Peach Ice Cream

## Ingredients:

1 (23½-ounce) jar sliced peaches, drained
⅓ cup sweetened almond milk creamer

2 tablespoons monk fruit sweetener
½ teaspoon vanilla bean powder

## Preparation:

1. In an empty Ninja CREAMi pint container, place the sliced peaches. 2. In a small-sized bowl, blend together the creamer, monk fruit sweetener and vanilla bean powder. 3. Pour the creamer mixture over the peaches. 4. Cover the container with storage lid and freeze for 24 hours. 5. After 24 hours, remove the lid from container and arrange into the outer bowl of Ninja CREAMi. 6. Install the "Creamerizer Paddle" onto the lid of outer bowl. 7. Then rotate the lid clockwise to lock. 8. Press "Power" button to turn on the unit. 9. Then press "ICE CREAM" button. 10. When the program is completed, turn the outer bowl and release it from the machine. 11. Transfer the ice cream into serving bowls and enjoy immediately.

**Nutritional Information per Serving:** Calories: 359 | Fat: 2.3g | Sat Fat: 0g | Carbohydrates: 84.5g | Fiber: 13.2g | Sugar: 84.5g | Protein: 8.1g

# Easy Coffee Ice Cream

## Ingredients:

1 cup hemp milk
¾ cup full-fat coconut milk
1 teaspoon vanilla extract

2 decaf instant coffee packets
5 tablespoons maple syrup

## Preparation:

1. In a bowl, add hemp milk and remaining ingredients and whisk until blended thoroughly. 2. Transfer the blended mixture into an empty Ninja CREAMi pint container. 3. Cover the container with storage lid and freeze for 24 hours. 4. After 24 hours, remove the lid from container and arrange into the outer bowl of Ninja CREAMi. 5. Install the "Creamerizer Paddle" onto the lid of outer bowl. 6. Then rotate the lid clockwise to lock. 7. Press "Power" button to turn on the unit. 8. Then press "ICE CREAM" button. 9. When the program is completed, turn the outer bowl and release it from the machine. 10. Transfer the ice cream into serving bowls and enjoy immediately.

**Nutritional Information per Serving:** Calories: 136 | Fat: 3.4g | Sat Fat: 2.3g | Carbohydrates: 25.8g | Fiber: 0.5g | Sugar: 20.8g | Protein: 0.9g

# Caramel Ice Cream

## Ingredients:

1 tablespoon cream cheese
⅓ cup granulated sugar
1 teaspoon vanilla extract
½ teaspoon salt

1 cup whole milk
¾ cup heavy cream
2 tablespoons caramel dip

## Preparation:

1. In a large-sized microwave-safe bowl, add the cream cheese and microwave on High for about 10 seconds. 2. Remove from the microwave and stir until smooth. 3. Add the sugar, vanilla extract and salt and with a wire whisk, beat until the mixture looks like frosting. 4. Slowly add the milk and heavy cream and whisk until blended thoroughly. 5. In a small-sized microwave-safe bowl, add the caramel dip and microwave on High for about 10-15 seconds. 6. Place the caramel dip into the bowl of milk mixture and mix well. 7. Transfer the blended mixture into an empty Ninja CREAMi pint container. 8. Cover the container with storage lid and freeze for 24 hours. 9. After 24 hours, remove the lid from container and arrange into the outer bowl of Ninja CREAMi. 10. Install the "Creamerizer Paddle" onto the lid of outer bowl. 11. Then rotate the lid clockwise to lock. 12. Press "Power" button to turn on the unit. 13. Then press "ICE CREAM" button. 14. When the program is completed, turn the outer bowl and release it from the machine. 15. Transfer the ice cream into serving bowls and enjoy immediately.

**Nutritional Information per Serving:** Calories: 218 | Fat: 11.9g | Sat Fat: 7.5g | Carbohydrates: 26.3g | Fiber: 0g | Sugar: 23.5g | Protein: 2.9g

# Pumpkin Marshmallow Ice Cream

Preparation Time: 15 minutes | Cooking Time: 25 seconds | Servings: 4

## Ingredients:

1 tablespoon cream cheese
⅓ cup granulated sugar
1 teaspoon vanilla extract
1 cup whole milk

¾ cup heavy cream
¼ cup pumpkin puree
7 large marshmallows

## Preparation:

1. In a large-sized microwave-safe bowl, add the cream cheese and microwave on High for about 10 seconds. 2. Remove from the microwave and stir until smooth. 3. Add the vanilla extract and sugar and with a wire whisk, beat until the mixture looks like frosting. 4. Slowly add the milk, heavy cream and pumpkin puree and whisk until blended thoroughly. 5. Meanwhile, with a handheld candle lighter, char the outside of each marshmallow. 6. Set aside to cool completely. 7. Carefully pull off the charred outside of each marshmallow. 8. In a small-sized microwave-safe bowl, place the insides of marshmallows and microwave for 15 seconds. 9. Place the marshmallow insides into the bowl of milk mixture and mix well. 10. Transfer the blended mixture into an empty Ninja CREAMi pint container. 11. Cover the container with storage lid and freeze for 24 hours. 12. After 24 hours, remove the lid from container and arrange into the outer bowl of Ninja CREAMi. 13. Install the "Creamerizer Paddle" onto the lid of outer bowl. 14. Then rotate the lid clockwise to lock. 15. Press "Power" button to turn on the unit. 16. Then press "ICE CREAM" button. 17. When the program is completed, turn the outer bowl and release it from the machine. 18. Transfer the ice cream into serving bowls and enjoy immediately.

**Nutritional Information per Serving:** Calories: 217 | Fat: 11.2g | Sat Fat: 6.9g | Carbohydrates: 27.2g | Fiber: 0g | Sugar: 24.1g | Protein: 2.7g

# Banana Coffee Creamer Ice Cream

## Ingredients:

2-3 ripe bananas, peeled and cut into 2-inch chunks
½ cup whole milk

½ cup sweet coffee creamer
1 teaspoon vanilla bean paste

## Preparation:

1. In a large-sized high-powered blender, add bananas and remaining ingredients and process until smooth. 2. Transfer the blended mixture into an empty Ninja CREAMi pint container. 3. Cover the container with storage lid and freeze for 24 hours. 4. After 24 hours, remove the lid from container and arrange into the outer bowl of Ninja CREAMi. 5. Install the "Creamerizer Paddle" onto the lid of outer bowl. 6. Then rotate the lid clockwise to lock. 7. Press "Power" button to turn on the unit. 8. Then press "ICE CREAM" button. 9. When the program is completed, turn the outer bowl and release it from the machine. 10. Transfer the ice cream into serving bowls and enjoy immediately.

**Nutritional Information per Serving:** Calories: 101 | Fat: 1.5g | Sat Fat: 0.8g | Carbohydrates: 22.3g | Fiber: 2.3g | Sugar: 13.2g | Protein: 1.9g

# Strawberry Vanilla Ice Cream

Preparation Time: 10 minutes | Servings: 4

## Ingredients:

¼ cup sugar
1 tablespoon cream cheese, softened
1 teaspoon vanilla bean paste

1 cup milk
¾ cup heavy whipping cream
6 medium fresh strawberries, hulled and quartered

## Preparation:

1. In a bowl, add the cream cheese, sugar, vanilla bean paste and with a wire whisk, mix until well combined. 2. Add in the milk and heavy whipping cream and beat until well combined. 3. Transfer the mixture into an empty Ninja CREAMi pint container. 4. Add the strawberry pieces and stir to combine. 5. Cover the container with storage lid and freeze for 24 hours. 6. After 24 hours, remove the lid from container and arrange into the Outer Bowl of Ninja CREAMi. 7. Install the Creamerizer Paddle onto the lid of Outer Bowl. 8. Then rotate the lid clockwise to lock. 9. Press Power button to turn on the unit. 10. Then press Ice Cream button. 11. When the program is completed, turn the Outer Bowl and release it from the machine. 12. Transfer the ice cream into serving bowls and serve immediately.

**Nutritional Information per Serving:** Calories: 175 | Fat: 10.5g | Sat Fat: 6.5g | Carbohydrates: 18.8g | Fiber: 0.4g | Sugar: 17.4g | Protein: 2.8g

# Chapter 4 Ice Cream Mix-Ins

# Coconut Pineapple Ice Cream

## Ingredients:

1¼ cups canned unsweetened coconut cream
½ cup canned pineapple tidbits

1 tablespoon coconut, toasted
1 tablespoon pineapple, chopped

## Preparation:

1. In an empty Ninja CREAMi pint container, place coconut cream and ½ cup of pineapple tidbits and stir to combine. 2. Cover the container with storage lid and freeze for 24 hours. 3. After 24 hours, remove the lid from container and arrange into the outer bowl of Ninja CREAMi. 4. Install the "Creamerizer Paddle" onto the lid of outer bowl. 5. Then rotate the lid clockwise to lock. 6. Press "Power" button to turn on the unit. 7. Then press "ICE CREAM" button. 8. When the program is completed, with a spoon, create a 1½-inch wide hole in the center that reaches the bottom of the pint container. 9. Add the coconut and chopped pineapple in the hole and press "MIX-IN" button. 10. When the program is completed, turn the outer bowl and release it from the machine. 11. Transfer the ice cream into serving bowls and enjoy immediately.

Nutritional Information per Serving: Calories: 188 | Fat: 18.3g | Sat Fat: 16.2g | Carbohydrates: 7.4g | Fiber: 2.1g | Sugar: 4.9g | Protein: 1.9g

# Delicious Pistachio Pudding Ice Cream

## Ingredients:

1 (3.4-ounce) box instant pistachio pudding mix
1½ cups whole milk

½ cup heavy whipping cream
¼ cup pistachios, chopped

## Preparation:

1. In a large-sized bowl, add pudding mix, milk and whipping cream and whisk until blended thoroughly. 2. Transfer the blended mixture into an empty Ninja CREAMi pint container. 3. Cover the container with storage lid and freeze for 24 hours. 4. After 24 hours, remove the lid from container and arrange into the outer bowl of Ninja CREAMi. 5. Install the "Creamerizer Paddle" onto the lid of outer bowl. 6. Then rotate the lid clockwise to lock. 7. Press "Power" button to turn on the unit. 8. Then press "ICE CREAM" button. 9. When the program is completed, with a spoon, create a 1½-inch wide hole in the center that reaches the bottom of the pint container. 10. Add the pistachios in the hole and press "MIX-IN" button. 11. When the program is completed, turn the outer bowl and release it from the machine. 12. Transfer the ice cream into serving bowls and enjoy immediately.

Nutritional Information per Serving: Calories: 213 | Fat: 10.3g | Sat Fat: 5.4g | Carbohydrates: 26.8g | Fiber: 1.3g | Sugar: 5.1g | Protein: 4g

# Almond & Chocolate Chips Ice Cream

## Ingredients:

1 cup milk
½ cup half-and-half
¼ cup almond milk creamer
½ teaspoon almond extract

1 tablespoon cream of coconut
1 teaspoon almonds, toasted and sliced
1 teaspoon coconut, toasted
1 teaspoon mini chocolate chips

## Preparation:

1. 1n an empty Ninja CREAMi pint container, place chocolate milk, half-and-half, creamer, almond extract and cream of coconut and stir to combine. 2. Cover the container with storage lid and freeze for 24 hours. 3. After 24 hours, remove the lid from container and arrange into the outer bowl of Ninja CREAMi. 4. Install the "Creamerizer Paddle" onto the lid of outer bowl. 5. Then rotate the lid clockwise to lock. 6. Press "Power" button to turn on the unit. 7. Then press "ICE CREAM" button. 8. When the program is completed, with a spoon, create a 1½-inch wide hole in the center that reaches the bottom of the pint container. 9. Add the almonds, coconut and chocolate chips in the hole and press "MIX-IN" button. 10. When the program is completed, turn the outer bowl and release it from the machine. 11. Transfer the ice cream into serving bowls and enjoy immediately.

**Nutritional Information per Serving:** Calories: 128 | Fat: 8.6g | Sat Fat: 5.7g | Carbohydrates: 8.6g | Fiber: 0.2g | Sugar: 6.8g | Protein: 3.3g

# Chocolate Kale Peppermint Ice Cream

## Ingredients:

½ cup frozen kale, thawed and squeezed dry
½ cup dark brown sugar
1 cup whole milk
1 teaspoon peppermint extract

3 tablespoons dark cocoa powder
⅓ cup heavy cream
8 striped peppermint candies, roughly chopped

## Preparation:

1. In a blender, combine the kale, sugar, milk, peppermint extract, and cocoa powder. Blend on high for 60 seconds or until smooth. 2. Pour the mixture into the Ninja CREAMi Pint. 3. Seal the pint with the lid and freeze for 24 hours. 4. Remove the lid and assemble the unit as per the user instructions. 5. Select the ICE CREAM program. 6.When the program is completed, use a spoon to create a 1½-inch wide hole in the center of the ice cream that reaches the bottom of the pint. 7. Add the chopped peppermint candy pieces to the hole and select the MIX-IN program. 8. When the program is complete, remove the outer bowl. 9. Serve in bowls.

**Nutritional Information per Serving:** Calories: 148 | Fat: 5g | Sat Fat: 3g | Carbohydrates: 22g | Fiber: 0.3g | Sugar: 20g | Protein: 2g

# Maple White Chocolate Raspberry Ice Cream

## Ingredients:

1 cup fresh raspberries
1 cup full-fat coconut milk
⅓ cup maple syrup

1 teaspoon vanilla extract
2 tablespoons cacao butter, melted
½ of white chocolate bar, chopped

## Preparation:

1. In a large-sized high-powered blender, add raspberries, milk, maple syrup, vanilla extract and cacao butter and process until smooth. 2. Transfer the blended mixture into an empty Ninja CREAMi pint container. 3. Cover the container with storage lid and freeze for 24 hours. 4. After 24 hours, remove the lid from container and arrange into the outer bowl of Ninja CREAMi. 5. Install the "Creamerizer Paddle" onto the lid of outer bowl. 6. Then rotate the lid clockwise to lock. 7. Press "Power" button to turn on the unit. 8. Then press "ICE CREAM" button. 9. When the program is completed, with a spoon, create a 1½-inch wide hole in the center that reaches the bottom of the pint container. 10. Add the chopped chocolate in the hole and press "MIX-IN" button. 11. When the program is completed, turn the outer bowl and release it from the machine. 12. Transfer the ice cream into serving bowls and enjoy immediately. 13. Transfer the ice cream into serving bowls and enjoy immediately.

**Nutritional Information per Serving:** Calories: 335 | Fat: 22.6g | Sat Fat: 17.4g | Carbohydrates: 31.8g | Fiber: 2g | Sugar: 26.5g | Protein: 2.3g

# Caramel Mocha Oreo Ice Cream

## Ingredients:

1 cup chocolate milk
6 tablespoons coffee syrup

¾ cup caramel almond creamer
4 chocolate Oreo cookies, crushed

## Preparation:

1. In an empty Ninja CREAMi pint container, add milk and coffee syrup and stir to blend. 2. Top with the caramel creamer. 3. Cover the container with storage lid and freeze for 24 hours. 4. After 24 hours, remove the lid from container and arrange into the outer bowl of Ninja CREAMi. 5. Install the "Creamerizer Paddle" onto the lid of outer bowl. 6. Then rotate the lid clockwise to lock. 7. Press "Power" button to turn on the unit. 8. Then press "ICE CREAM" button. 9. When the program is completed, with a spoon, create a 1½-inch wide hole in the center that reaches the bottom of the pint container. 10. Add the crushed Oreos in the hole and press "MIX-IN" button. 11. When the program is completed, turn the outer bowl and release it from the machine. 12. Transfer the ice cream into serving bowls and enjoy immediately.

**Nutritional Information per Serving:** Calories: 230 | Fat: 4g | Sat Fat: 1.7g | Carbohydrates: 44.4g | Fiber: 0.8g | Sugar: 40.8g | Protein: 2.5g

# Strawberry Oreo Ice Cream

## Ingredients:

1 tablespoon cream cheese, softened

⅓ cup granulated sugar

1 teaspoon vanilla extract

6 strawberries, chopped

¾ cup heavy cream, whipped

1 cup whole milk

6 Oreos, broken

## Preparation:

1. Microwave the cream cheese for 10 seconds in a large microwave-safe bowl. 2. Combine the sugar and vanilla extract in a mixing bowl and whisk or scrape together until the mixture resembles frosting, about 60 seconds. 3. Slowly whisk in the heavy cream, chopped strawberries, and milk until smooth, and the sugar has dissolved. 4. Transfer the mixture into a Ninja Creami pint. 5. Cover the container with a pint lid and freeze for 24 hours. 6. Remove the lid from the container after 24 hours and arrange it into the outer bowl of Ninja Creami. 7. Install the "Creamerizer Paddle" onto the lid of the outer bowl. 8. Then rotate the lid clockwise to lock. 9. Turn on the unit. 10. Then select the "ICE CREAM" function. 11. When the program is completed, with a spoon, create a 1½-inch wide hole in the center that reaches the bottom of the pint. 12. Add the broken Oreos to the hole and select the "MIX-IN" function. 13. When the program is completed, turn the outer bowl and release it from the machine. 14. Serve in bowls.

**Nutritional Information per Serving:** Calories: 188 | Fat: 11g | Sat Fat: 6g | Carbohydrates: 20g | Fiber: 0g | Sugar: 20g | Protein: 2g

# Chocolate and Sugar Cookie Ice Cream

## Ingredients:

1 tablespoon cream cheese, at room temperature

2 tablespoons unsweetened cocoa powder

½ teaspoon stevia sweetener

3 tablespoons raw agave nectar

1 teaspoon vanilla extract

¾ cup heavy cream

1 cup whole milk

¼ cup reduced-fat sugar cookies, crushed

## Preparation:

1. In a big microwave-safe bowl, microwave the cream cheese for 10 seconds. Stir in the cocoa powder, stevia, agave, and vanilla. 2. Microwave for 60 seconds more, or until the mixture resembles frosting. Slowly whisk in the heavy cream and milk until the sugar has dissolved and the mixture is entirely mixed. 3. Transfer the mixture to the Ninja CREAMi Pint. 4. Snap the lid on the pint and freeze it for 24 hours. 5. Remove the lid and assemble the unit as per the user instructions. 6. Select the ICE CREAM program. 7. When the program is complete, use a spoon to create a 1½-inch wide hole in the center of the ice cream that reaches the bottom of the pint. 8. Add the crushed cookies to the hole and select the MIX-IN program. 9. When the program is complete, remove the outer bowl. 10. Serve in bowls.

**Nutritional Information per Serving:** Calories: 133 | Fat: 11g | Sat Fat: 7g | Carbohydrates: 5g | Fiber: 1.3g | Sugar: 3g | Protein: 3g

# Maple Walnut Ice Cream

## Ingredients:

1 tablespoon cream cheese, softened
⅓ cup granulated sugar
1 teaspoon maple extract

¾ cup heavy cream
1 cup whole milk
¼ cup walnuts, chopped, for mix-in

## Preparation:

1. Microwave the cream cheese for 10 seconds in a large microwave-safe bowl. Add the sugar and maple extract and combine with a whisk or rubber spatula for about 60 seconds, or until the mixture forms frosting. 2. Slowly whisk in the heavy cream and milk until smooth, and the sugar has dissolved. 3. Transfer the mixture to the Ninja CREAMi Pint. 4. Snap the lid on the pint and freeze it for 24 hours. 5. Remove the lid and assemble the unit as per the user instructions. 6. Select the ICE CREAM program. 7. When the program is complete, use a spoon to create a 1½-inch wide hole in the center of the ice cream that reaches the bottom of the pint. 8. Add the chopped walnuts to the hole and select the MIX-IN program. 9. When the program is complete, remove the outer bowl. 10. Serve in bowls.

**Nutritional Information per Serving:** Calories: 237 | Fat: 15g | Sat Fat: 7g | Carbohydrates: 21g | Fiber: 0.5g | Sugar: 20g | Protein: 4g

# Vegan Chocolate Chip Ice Cream

## Ingredients:

½ cup sugar
1 cup coconut milk
1 cup cashew milk
1 teaspoon vanilla extract

¼ teaspoon salt
1-ounce vegan chocolate chips
2 teaspoons coconut oil

## Preparation:

1. Combine the sugar, cashew milk, and coconut milk in a medium saucepan over medium heat, stirring with a whisk until the sugar has dissolved. 2. Whisk in the vanilla and salt until well combined. 3. Transfer the mixture to the Ninja CREAMi Pint. 4. Snap the lid on the pint and freeze it for 24 hours. 5. Remove the lid and assemble the unit as per the user instructions. 6. Select the ICE CREAM program. 7. Combine the chocolate chips and coconut oil in a medium saucepan. Cook, whisking constantly until the chips have melted. 8. Allow the chocolate mixture to cool to around 80°F. 9. When the program is complete, use a spoon to create a 1½-inch wide hole in the center of the ice cream that reaches the bottom of the pint. 10. Add the chocolate mixture to the hole and select the MIX-IN program. 11. When the program is complete, remove the outer bowl. 12. Serve in bowls.

**Nutritional Information per Serving:** Calories: 324 | Fat: 20g | Sat Fat: 13g | Carbohydrates: 26g | Fiber: 2g | Sugar: 28g | Protein: 2g

# Lavender Wafer Cookie Ice Cream

## Ingredients:

¾ cup heavy cream
1 tablespoon dried culinary lavender
⅛ teaspoon salt
¾ cup whole milk

½ cup sweetened condensed milk
4 drops purple food coloring
⅓ cup chocolate wafer cookies, crushed

## Preparation:

1. In a medium saucepan, add the heavy cream, lavender and salt and mix well. 2. Place the saucepan over low heat and steep, covered for about ten minutes, stirring after every two minutes. 3. Remove from the heat and through a fine-mesh strainer, strain the cream mixture into a large bowl. 4. Discard the lavender leaves. 5. In the bowl of cream mixture, add the milk, condensed milk and purple food coloring and beat until smooth. 6. Transfer the mixture into an empty Ninja CREAMi pint container. 7. Cover the container with storage lid and freeze for 24 hours. 8. After 24 hours, remove the lid from container and arrange into the Outer Bowl of Ninja CREAMi. 9. Install the Creamerizer Paddle onto the lid of Outer Bowl. 10. Then rotate the lid clockwise to lock. 11. Press Power button to turn on the unit. 12. Then press Ice Cream button. 13. When the program is completed, with a spoon, create a 1½-inch wide hole in the center that reaches the bottom of the pint container. 14. Add the crushed cookies the hole and press Mix-In button. 15. When the program is completed, turn the Outer Bowl and release it from the machine. 16. Transfer the ice cream into serving bowls and serve immediately.

Nutritional Information per Serving: Calories: 229 | Fat: 13.2g | Sat Fat: 8.1g | Carbohydrates: 23.5g | Fiber: 0g | Sugar: 23.2g | Protein: 5g

# Delicious Chocolate Spinach Ice Cream

## Ingredients:

½ cup frozen spinach, thawed and squeezed dry
1 cup whole milk
½ cup granulated sugar
1 teaspoon mint extract

3-5 drops green food coloring
⅓ cup heavy cream
¼ cup chocolate chunks, chopped
¼ cup brownie, cut into 1-inch pieces

## Preparation:

1. In a high-speed blender, add the spinach, milk, sugar, mint extract and food coloring and pulse until mixture smooth. 2. Transfer the mixture into an empty Ninja CREAMi pint container. 3. Add the heavy cream and stir until well combined. 4. Cover the container with storage lid and freeze for 24 hours. 5. After 24 hours, remove the lid from container and arrange into the Outer Bowl of Ninja CREAMi. 6. Install the Creamerizer Paddle onto the lid of Outer Bowl. 7. Then rotate the lid clockwise to lock. 8. Press Power button to turn on the unit. 9. Then press Ice Cream button. 10. When the program is completed, with a spoon, create a 1½-inch wide hole in the center that reaches the bottom of the pint container. 11. Add the chocolate chunks and brownie pieces into the hole and press Mix-In button. 12. When the program is completed, turn the Outer Bowl and release it from the machine. 13. Transfer the ice cream into serving bowls and serve immediately.

Nutritional Information per Serving: Calories: 243 | Fat: 10.1g | Sat Fat: 6g | Carbohydrates: 36.7g | Fiber: 0.4g | Sugar: 33.7g | Protein: 3.4g

# Blueberry & Graham Cracker Ice Cream

## Ingredients:

1 cup fresh blueberries
¼ cup plus 1 teaspoon sugar, divided
½ teaspoon lemon juice
1 cup milk
½ cup half-and-half

2 tablespoons instant vanilla pudding mix
1 graham cracker, crushed
1 teaspoon butter, melted
¼ teaspoon ground cinnamon

## Preparation:

1. For pie filling: In a small saucepan, combine the blueberries, ¼ cup of sugar, and lemon juice. Cook over medium heat for about 5 minutes, stirring constantly, until the sugar dissolves. 2. Remove the pan of filling from heat and set aside to cool. 3. In an empty Ninja CREAMi pint container, place milk, half-and-half and pudding mix and with a wire whisk, beat until blended thoroughly. 4. Add the filling mixture and mix well. 5. Cover the container with storage lid and freeze for 24 hours. 6. After 24 hours, remove the lid from container and arrange into the outer bowl of Ninja CREAMi. 7. Install the "Creamerizer Paddle" onto the lid of outer bowl. 8. Then rotate the lid clockwise to lock. 9. Press "Power" button to turn on the unit. 10. Then press "ICE CREAM" button. 11. Meanwhile, in a medium-sized bowl, add graham cracker, butter, remaining sugar and cinnamon and mix well. 12. When the program is completed, with a spoon, create a 1½-inch wide hole in the center that reaches the bottom of the pint container. 13. Add the cracker mixture in the hole and press "MIX-IN" button. 14. When the program is completed, turn the outer bowl and release it from the machine. 15. Transfer the ice cream into serving bowls and enjoy immediately.

**Nutritional Information per Serving:** Calories: 177 | Fat: 7.2g | Sat Fat: 4.1g | Carbohydrates: 26.4g | Fiber: 1.1g | Sugar: 22.1g | Protein: 3.7g

# Raisin Rum Ice Cream

## Ingredients:

3 large egg yolks
¼ cup dark brown sugar (or coconut sugar)
1 tablespoon light corn syrup
½ cup heavy cream

1 cup whole milk
1 teaspoon rum extract
⅓ cup raisins
¼ cup dark or spiced rum

## Preparation:

1. In a small saucepan, combine the egg yolks, sugar, and corn syrup. Whisk until everything is well mixed and the sugar has dissolved. Whisk together the heavy cream and milk until smooth. 2. Stir the mixture frequently with a whisk or a rubber spatula in a saucepan over medium-low heat. Using an instant-read thermometer, cook until the temperature hits 165°F–175°F. 3. Remove the base from heat, stir in the rum extract, then pour through a fine-mesh strainer into an empty CREAMi Pint. Place into an ice bath. After cooling, cover the Pint with the storage lid and freeze for 24 hours. 4. While the base is cooling, prepare the mix-in. Add the raisins and rum to a small bowl and microwave for 1 minute. Let cool, then drain the remaining rum. Cover and set aside. 5. Remove the Pint from the freezer and remove its lid. Place the Pint in the outer bowl, install the Creamerizer Paddle onto the outer bowl lid, and lock the lid assembly on the outer bowl. Select ICE CREAM. 6. With a spoon, create a 1½-inch wide hole that reaches the bottom of the Pint. Add the mixed raisins to the hole and process again using the MIX-IN program. 7. When processing is complete, remove the ice cream from the Pint.

**Nutritional Information per Serving:** Calories 160 | Protein 2g | Carbohydrate 18g | Dietary Fiber 1g | Sugar 18g | Fat 7g | Sodium 45mg

# Blueberry & Graham Cracker Ice Cream

## Ingredients:

1 cup fresh blueberries

¼ cup plus 1 teaspoon sugar, divided

½ teaspoon lemon juice

1 cup milk

½ cup half-and-half

2 tablespoons instant vanilla pudding mix

1 graham cracker, crushed

1 teaspoon butter, melted

¼ teaspoon ground cinnamon

## Preparation:

1. For pie filling: In a small saucepan, combine the blueberries, ¼ cup of sugar, and lemon juice. Cook over medium heat for about 5 minutes, stirring constantly, until the sugar dissolves. 2. Remove the pan of filling from heat and set aside to cool. 3. In an empty Ninja CREAMi pint container, place milk, half-and-half and pudding mix and with a wire whisk, beat until blended thoroughly. 4. Add the filling mixture and mix well. 5. Cover the container with storage lid and freeze for 24 hours. 6. After 24 hours, remove the lid from container and arrange into the outer bowl of Ninja CREAMi. 7. Install the "Creamerizer Paddle" onto the lid of outer bowl. 8. Then rotate the lid clockwise to lock. 9. Press "Power" button to turn on the unit. 10. Then press "ICE CREAM" button. 11. Meanwhile, in a medium-sized bowl, add graham cracker, butter, remaining sugar and cinnamon and mix well. 12. When the program is completed, with a spoon, create a 1½-inch wide hole in the center that reaches the bottom of the pint container. 13. Add the cracker mixture in the hole and press "MIX-IN" button. 14. When the program is completed, turn the outer bowl and release it from the machine. 15. Transfer the ice cream into serving bowls and enjoy immediately.

**Nutritional Information per Serving:** Calories: 177 | Fat: 7.2g | Sat Fat: 4.1g | Carbohydrates: 26.4g | Fiber: 1.1g | Sugar: 22.1g | Protein: 3.7g

# Mint Chocolate Ice Cream

## Ingredients:

½ cup fresh mint leaves

⅓ cup plus 1 teaspoon maple syrup, divided

1 cup whole milk

¾ cup heavy cream

¼ cup dark chocolate chips

## Preparation:

1. In a large-sized bowl, place mint leaves and 1 teaspoon of maple syrup and with a muddler, muddle until liquid forms. 2. Add in the milk, heavy cream and maple remaining syrup and whisk until blended thoroughly. 3. Through a fine mesh strainer, strain the mixture into an empty Ninja CREAMi pint container. 4. Cover the container with storage lid and freeze for 24 hours. 5. After 24 hours, remove the lid from container and arrange into the outer bowl of Ninja CREAMi. 6. Install the "Creamerizer Paddle" onto the lid of outer bowl. 7. Then rotate the lid clockwise to lock. 8. Press "Power" button to turn on the unit. 9. Then press "ICE CREAM" button. 10. When the program is completed, with a spoon, create a 1½-inch wide hole in the center that reaches the bottom of the pint container. 11. Add the chocolate chips in the hole and press "MIX-IN" button. 12. When the program is completed, turn the outer bowl and release it from the machine. 13. Transfer the ice cream into serving bowls and enjoy immediately.

**Nutritional Information per Serving:** Calories: 223 | Fat: 12.4g | Sat Fat: 7.6g | Carbohydrates: 27g | Fiber: 0.8g | Sugar: 22.9g | Protein: 3.3g

# Fresh Blueberry & Banana Ice Cream

## Ingredients:

⅔ cup coconut cream
¼ cup maple syrup
1 tablespoon mayonnaise
½ tablespoon fresh lemon juice

½ tablespoon vanilla extract
6 ounces fresh blueberries
1 small banana, peeled and sliced
¼ cup graham cracker crumbs

## Preparation:

1. In a large-sized bowl, add coconut cream, maple syrup, mayonnaise, lemon juice and vanilla extract, whisk until the mixture looks like frosting with a wire whisk. 2. Add the blueberries and banana slices and stir to blend. 3. Transfer the blended mixture into an empty Ninja CREAMi pint container. 4. Place the container into an ice bath to cool. 5. After cooling, cover the container with the storage lid and freeze for 24 hours. 6. After 24 hours, remove the lid from container and arrange into the outer bowl of Ninja CREAMi. 7. Install the "Creamerizer Paddle" onto the lid of outer bowl. 8. Then rotate the lid clockwise to lock. 9. Press "Power" button to turn on the unit. 10. Then press "ICE CREAM" button. 11. When the program is completed, with a spoon, create a 1½-inch wide hole in the center that reaches the bottom of the pint container. 12. Add the graham cracker crumbs in the hole and press "MIX-IN" button. 13. When the program is completed, turn the outer bowl and release it from the machine. 14. Transfer the ice cream into serving bowls and enjoy immediately.

**Nutritional Information per Serving:** Calories: 232 | Fat: 11.6g | Sat Fat: 8.8g | Carbohydrates: 32.5g | Fiber: 2.7g | Sugar: 22.5g | Protein: 1.9g

# Chocolate Coffee Banana Ice Cream

## Ingredients:

¾ cup oat milk
½ cup coconut cream
5 tablespoons maple syrup
1½ tablespoons instant coffee

1½ teaspoons vanilla extract
½ cup bananas, peeled and sliced
¼ cup chocolate shavings

## Preparation:

1. In a large-sized bowl, add oat milk, coconut cream, maple syrup, coffee and vanilla extract. With a wire whisk, whisk until the mixture looks like frosting. 2. Add banana slices and stir to blend. 3. Transfer the blended mixture into an empty Ninja CREAMi pint container. 4. Place the container into an ice bath to cool. 5. After cooling, cover the container with the storage lid and freeze for 24 hours. 6. After 24 hours, remove the lid from container and arrange into the outer bowl of Ninja CREAMi. 7. Install the "Creamerizer Paddle" onto the lid of outer bowl. 8. Then rotate the lid clockwise to lock. 9. Press "Power" button to turn on the unit. 10. Then press "ICE CREAM" button. 11. When the program is completed, with a spoon, create a 1½-inch wide hole in the center that reaches the bottom of the pint container. 12. Add the chocolate shavings in the hole and press "MIX-IN" button. 13. When the program is completed, turn the outer bowl and release it from the machine. 14. Transfer the ice cream into serving bowls and enjoy immediately.

**Nutritional Information per Serving:** Calories: 236 | Fat: 10.8g | Sat Fat: 8.6g | Carbohydrates: 33.7g | Fiber: 1.9g | Sugar: 27.3g | Protein: 2.5g

# Banana Pudding Oreo Ice Cream

## Ingredients:

½ cup coconut cream

½ cup oat milk

¼ cup dry instant banana pudding mix

2 tablespoons granulated sugar

1 tablespoon cream cheese, softened

1½ teaspoons vanilla extract

⅔ cup banana, peeled and sliced

3 golden Oreo cookies, crushed

## Preparation:

1. In a large-sized bowl, add coconut cream, oat milk, pudding mix, sugar, cream cheese and vanilla extract and with a wire whisk, whisk until the mixture looks like frosting. 2. Add banana slices and stir to blend. 3. Transfer the blended mixture into an empty Ninja CREAMi pint container. 4. Place the container into an ice bath to cool. 5. After cooling, cover the container with the storage lid and freeze for 24 hours. 6. After 24 hours, remove the lid from container and arrange into the outer bowl of Ninja CREAMi. 7. Install the "Creamerizer Paddle" onto the lid of outer bowl. 8. Then rotate the lid clockwise to lock. 9. Press "Power" button to turn on the unit. 10. Then press "ICE CREAM" button. 11. When the program is completed, with a spoon, create a 1½-inch wide hole in the center that reaches the bottom of the pint container. 12. Add the crushed Oreos in the hole and press "MIX-IN" button. 13. When the program is completed, turn the outer bowl and release it from the machine. 14. Transfer the ice cream into serving bowls and enjoy immediately.

**Nutritional Information per Serving:** Calories: 171 | Fat: 10g | Sat Fat: 7.3g | Carbohydrates: 19.1g | Fiber: 1.1g | Sugar: 12.6g | Protein: 2.2g

# Goat Cheese & Almond Ice Cream

## Ingredients:

1 cup heavy cream
½ cup whole milk
¼ cup honey
2 ounces goat cheese

2 tablespoons blackberry jam
2 tablespoons lemon curd
¼ cup almonds, toasted and chopped

## Preparation:

1. In a small-sized saucepan, add cream, milk, and honey over medium heat and cook until heated through, stirring continuously. 2. Add in the goat cheese and stir until blended thoroughly. 3. Transfer the blended mixture into an empty Ninja CREAMi pint container. 4. Place the container into an ice bath to cool. 5. After cooling, cover the container with the storage lid and freeze for 24 hours. 6. After 24 hours, remove the lid from container and arrange into the outer bowl of Ninja CREAMi. 7. Install the "Creamerizer Paddle" onto the lid of outer bowl. 8. Then rotate the lid clockwise to lock. 9. Press "Power" button to turn on the unit. 10. Then press "ICE CREAM" button. 11. When the program is completed, with a spoon, create a 1½-inch wide hole in the center that reaches the bottom of the pint container. 12. Add the jam, lemon curd and almonds in the hole and press "MIX-IN" button. 13. When the program is completed, turn the outer bowl and release it from the machine. 14. Transfer the ice cream into serving bowls and enjoy immediately.

**Nutritional Information per Serving:** Calories: 340 | Fat: 23.1g | Sat Fat: 12.7g | Carbohydrates: 29.8g | Fiber: 0.8g | Sugar: 27.6g | Protein: 7.7g

# Chocolate Cookies Ice Cream

## Ingredients:

1 tablespoon cream cheese
⅓ cup granulated sugar
1 teaspoon vanilla extract

1 cup whole milk
¾ cup heavy cream
3 chocolate sandwich cookies, broken

## Preparation:

1. In a large-sized microwave-safe bowl, add the cream cheese and microwave on High for about 10 seconds. 2. Take it out of the microwave and stir until smooth. 3. Add the sugar and vanilla extract, then whisk with a wire whisk until the mixture resembles frosting. 4. Slowly add the milk and heavy cream and whisk until blended thoroughly. 5. Transfer the blended mixture into an empty Ninja CREAMi pint container. 6. Cover the container with storage lid and freeze for 24 hours. 7. After 24 hours, remove the lid from container and arrange into the outer bowl of Ninja CREAMi. 8. Install the "Creamerizer Paddle" onto the lid of outer bowl. 9. Then rotate the lid clockwise to lock. 10. Press "Power" button to turn on the unit. Then press "ICE CREAM" button. 11. When the program is completed, with a spoon, create a 1½-inch wide hole in the center that reaches the bottom of the pint container. 12. Add the crushed cookies in the hole and press "MIX-IN" button. 13. When the program is completed, turn the outer bowl and release it from the machine. 14. Transfer the ice cream into serving bowls and enjoy immediately.

**Nutritional Information per Serving:** Calories: 271 | Fat: 14.9g | Sat Fat: 7.6g | Carbohydrates: 33.8g | Fiber: 0g | Sugar: 20g | Protein: 3.4g

# Lemon Oreo Ice Cream

## Ingredients:

1 tablespoon cream cheese, softened
⅓ cup granulated sugar
1 teaspoon lemon extract

1 cup whole milk
¾ cup heavy cream
3-4 golden Oreo cookies, crushed

## Preparation:

1. In a large-sized microwave-safe bowl, add the cream cheese and microwave on High for about 10 seconds. 2. Remove from the microwave and stir until smooth. 3. Add the sugar and lemon extract and with a wire whisk, whisk until the mixture looks like frosting. 4. Slowly add the milk and heavy cream and whisk until blended thoroughly. 5. Transfer the blended mixture into an empty Ninja CREAMi pint container. 6. Cover the container with storage lid and freeze for 24 hours. 7. After 24 hours, remove the lid from container and arrange into the outer bowl of Ninja CREAMi. 8. Install the "Creamerizer Paddle" onto the lid of outer bowl. 9. Then rotate the lid clockwise to lock. 10. Press "Power" button to turn on the unit. 11. Then press "ICE CREAM" button. 12. When the program is completed, with a spoon, create a 1½-inch wide hole in the center that reaches the bottom of the pint container. 13. Add the crushed Oreos in the hole and press "MIX-IN" button. 14. When the program is completed, turn the outer bowl and release it from the machine. 15. Transfer the ice cream into serving bowls and enjoy immediately.

**Nutritional Information per Serving:** Calories: 223 | Fat: 12.6g | Sat Fat: 7.2g | Carbohydrates: 25.6g | Fiber: 0.2g | Sugar: 23.1g | Protein: 3g

# Tasty Apple Pie Ice Cream

## Ingredients:

1 tablespoon cream cheese, softened
2 tablespoons brown sugar
¾ teaspoon apple pie spice
½ cup heavy cream

¼ cup whole milk
1 cup canned apple pie filling
¼-½ cup graham crackers, chopped

## Preparation:

1. In a large-sized microwave-safe bowl, add the cream cheese and microwave on High for about 10 seconds. 2. Remove from the microwave and stir until smooth. 3. Add the brown sugar and apple pie spice and with a wire whisk, whisk until the mixture looks like frosting. 4. In a separate large-sized bowl, add heavy cream, milk, and apple pie filling and with an immersion blender, whip until apples are chopped into small pieces. 5. Gradually add the milk mixture into the bowl of sugar mixture and whisk until blended thoroughly. 6. Transfer the blended mixture into an empty Ninja CREAMi pint container. 7. Place the container into an ice bath to cool. 8. After cooling, cover the container with the storage lid and freeze for 24 hours. 9. After 24 hours, remove the lid from container and arrange into the outer bowl of Ninja CREAMi. 10. Install the "Creamerizer Paddle" onto the lid of outer bowl. 11. Then rotate the lid clockwise to lock. 12. Press "Power" button to turn on the unit. 13. Then press "ICE CREAM" button. 14. When the program is completed, with a spoon, create a 1½-inch wide hole in the center that reaches the bottom of the pint container. 15. Add the chopped graham crackers in the hole and press "MIX-IN" button. 16. When the program is completed, turn the outer bowl and release it from the machine. 17. Transfer the ice cream into serving bowls and enjoy immediately.

**Nutritional Information per Serving:** Calories: 201 | Fat: 7.5g | Sat Fat: 4.4g | Carbohydrates: 31.8g | Fiber: 0.9g | Sugar: 22g | Protein: 1.4g

# Special Tiramisu Ice Cream

## Ingredients:

⅓ cup granulated sugar
½ tablespoon instant espresso powder
½ teaspoon unsweetened cocoa powder
1 tablespoon mascarpone cheese
1 teaspoon vanilla extract

1 cup whole milk
¾ cup heavy cream
1 tablespoon spiced rum
3-4 shortbread cookies, crushed

## Preparation:

1. In a large-sized bowl, add sugar, espresso powder, cocoa powder, mascarpone cheese and vanilla extract and whisk until blended thoroughly. 2. Add milk and heavy cream and whisk until blended thoroughly. 3. Add rum and whisk until blended thoroughly. 4. Transfer the blended mixture into an empty Ninja CREAMi pint container. 5. Place the container into an ice bath to cool. 6. After cooling, cover the container with the storage lid and freeze for 24 hours. 7. After 24 hours, remove the lid from container and arrange into the outer bowl of Ninja CREAMi. 8. Install the "Creamerizer Paddle" onto the lid of outer bowl. 9. Then rotate the lid clockwise to lock. 10. Press "Power" button to turn on the unit. 11. Then press "ICE CREAM" button. 12. When the program is completed, with a spoon, create a 1½-inch wide hole in the center that reaches the bottom of the pint container. 13. Add the crushed cookies in the hole and press "MIX-IN" button. 14. When the program is completed, turn the outer bowl and release it from the machine. 15. Transfer the ice cream into serving bowls and enjoy immediately.

**Nutritional Information per Serving:** Calories: 338 | Fat: 19.8g | Sat Fat: 11.9g | Carbohydrates: 34.7g | Fiber: 0.1g | Sugar: 26.8g | Protein: 4.4g

# Homemade Mint Chocolate Cookies Ice Cream

## Ingredients:

¾ cup coconut cream
¼ cup monk fruit sweetener with Erythritol
2 tablespoons agave nectar
½ teaspoon mint extract

5-6 drops green food coloring
1 cup oat milk
3 chocolate sandwich cookies, quartered

## Preparation:

1. In a large bowl, add the coconut cream and beat until smooth. 2. Add the sweetener, agave nectar, mint extract and food coloring and beat until sweetener is dissolved. 3. Add the oat milk and beat until well combined. 4. Transfer the mixture into an empty Ninja CREAMi pint container. 5. Cover the container with storage lid and freeze for 24 hours. 6. After 24 hours, remove the lid from container and arrange into the Outer Bowl of Ninja CREAMi. 7. Install the Creamerizer Paddle onto the lid of Outer Bowl. 8. Then rotate the lid clockwise to lock. 9. Press Power button to turn on the unit. 10. Then press Lite Ice Cream button. 11. When the program is completed, with a spoon, create a 1½-inch wide hole in the center that reaches the bottom of the pint container. 12. Add the cookie pieces into the hole and press Mix-In button. 13. When the program is completed, turn the Outer Bowl and release it from the machine. 14. Transfer the ice cream into serving bowls and serve immediately.

**Nutritional Information per Serving:** Calories: 201 | Fat: 12.8g | Sat Fat: 9.8g | Carbohydrates: 21.9g | Fiber: 2.2g | Sugar: 16.8g | Protein: 2.4g

# Chapter 5 Sorbets

# Refreshing Lemon Sorbet

## Ingredients:

1 cup warm water

½ cup fresh lemon juice

¼ cup trehalose sugar

1 tablespoon agave nectar

## Preparation:

1. In a large-sized bowl, add water and remaining ingredients and whisk until blended thoroughly. 2. Transfer the blended mixture into an empty Ninja CREAMi pint container. 3. Cover the container with storage lid and freeze for 24 hours. 4. After 24 hours, remove the lid from container and arrange into the outer bowl of Ninja CREAMi. 5. Install the "Creamerizer Paddle" onto the lid of outer bowl. 6. Then rotate the lid clockwise to lock. 7. Press "Power" button to turn on the unit. 8. Then press "SORBET" button. 9. When the program is completed, turn the outer bowl and release it from the machine. 10. Transfer the sorbet into serving bowls and enjoy immediately.

**Nutritional Information per Serving:** Calories: 69 | Fat: 0.2g | Sat Fat: 0.2g | Carbohydrates: 17.1g | Fiber: 0.4g | Sugar: 16.9g | Protein: 0.2g

# Simple Orange Sorbet

## Ingredients:

1 (20-ounce) can mandarin oranges with liquid

## Preparation:

1. Place the orange pieces into an empty Ninja CREAMi container to the MAX FILL line. 2. Cover the orange pieces with liquid from the can. 3. Cover the container with storage lid and freeze for 24 hours. 4. After 24 hours, remove the lid from container and arrange into the outer bowl of Ninja CREAMi. 5. Install the "Creamerizer Paddle" onto the lid of outer bowl. 6. Then rotate the lid clockwise to lock. 7. Press "Power" button to turn on the unit. 8. Then press "SORBET" button. 9. When the program is completed, turn the outer bowl and release it from the machine. 10. Transfer the sorbet into serving bowls and enjoy immediately.

**Nutritional Information per Serving:** Calories: 52 | Fat: 0g | Sat Fat: 0g | Carbohydrates: 13.6g | Fiber: 1g | Sugar: 12.6g | Protein: 0.9g

# Lime Mango Sorbet

## Ingredients:

¾ cup margarita mix
3 tablespoons gold tequila
2 tablespoons fresh lime juice
1 tablespoon agave nectar

¼ teaspoon cayenne powder
¼ teaspoon salt
1 (15-ounce) can mango chunks

## Preparation:

1. In a bowl, add margarita mix and remaining ingredients except for mango chunks and whisk until blended thoroughly. 2. Add mango chunks and toss to coat. 3. Transfer the blended mixture into an empty Ninja CREAMi pint container. 4. Cover the container with storage lid and freeze for 24 hours. 5. After 24 hours, remove the lid from container and arrange into the outer bowl of Ninja CREAMi. 6. Install the "Creamerizer Paddle" onto the lid of outer bowl. 7. Then rotate the lid clockwise to lock. 8. Press "Power" button to turn on the unit. 9. Then press "SORBET" button. 10. When the program is completed, turn the outer bowl and release it from the machine. 11. Transfer the sorbet into serving bowls and enjoy immediately.

**Nutritional Information per Serving:** Calories: 132 | Fat: 0.4g | Sat Fat: 0g | Carbohydrates: 27g | Fiber: 2g | Sugar: 24.3g | Protein: 0.9g

# Cherry Cola Rum Sorbet

## Ingredients:

1½ cups cola
⅓ cup maraschino cherries
⅓ cup spiced rum

¼ cup water
1 tablespoon fresh lime juice

## Preparation:

1. In a high-powered blender, add cola and remaining ingredients and process until smooth. 2. Transfer the blended mixture into an empty Ninja CREAMi pint container. 3. Cover the container with storage lid and freeze for 24 hours. 4. After 24 hours, remove the lid from container and arrange into the outer bowl of Ninja CREAMi. 5. Install the "Creamerizer Paddle" onto the lid of outer bowl. 6. Then rotate the lid clockwise to lock. 7. Press "Power" button to turn on the unit. 8. Then press "SORBET" button. 9. When the program is completed, turn the outer bowl and release it from the machine. 10. Transfer the sorbet into serving bowls and enjoy immediately.

**Nutritional Information per Serving:** Calories: 95 | Fat: 0.1g | Sat Fat: 0g | Carbohydrates: 13.4g | Fiber: 0.3g | Sugar: 12.5g | Protein: 0.2g

# Easy Strawberry Sorbet

## Ingredients:

2 cups fresh strawberry puree

¼ cup granulated sugar

1 tablespoon whole milk

## Preparation:

1. In a medium-sized bowl, add strawberry puree, sugar and milk and whisk until blended thoroughly. 2. Transfer the blended mixture into an empty Ninja CREAMi pint container. 3. Cover the container with storage lid and freeze for 24 hours. 4. After 24 hours, remove the lid from container and arrange into the outer bowl of Ninja CREAMi. 5. Install the "Creamerizer Paddle" onto the lid of outer bowl. Then rotate the lid clockwise to lock. 6. Press "Power" button to turn on the unit. 7. Then press "SORBET" button. 8. When the program is completed, turn the outer bowl and release it from the machine. 9. Transfer the sorbet into serving bowls and enjoy immediately.

**Nutritional Information per Serving:** Calories: 72 | Fat: 0.3g | Sat Fat: 0.1g | Carbohydrates: 18.2g | Fiber: 1.4g | Sugar: 16.2g | Protein: 0.6g

# Lime Blackberry Sorbet

## Ingredients:

3 cups fresh blackberries

5 ounces simple syrup

6 tablespoons fresh lime juice

## Preparation:

1. In an empty Ninja CREAMi pint container, add raspberries, maple syrup and lime juice and mix well. 2. Cover the container with storage lid and freeze for 24 hours. 3. After 24 hours, remove the lid from container and arrange into the outer bowl of Ninja CREAMi. 4. Install the "Creamerizer Paddle" onto the lid of outer bowl. 5. Then rotate the lid clockwise to lock. 6. Press "Power" button to turn on the unit. 7. Then press "SORBET" button. 8. When the program is completed, turn the outer bowl and release it from the machine. 9. Transfer the sorbet into serving bowls and enjoy immediately.

**Nutritional Information per Serving:** Calories: 162 | Fat: 0.5g | Sat Fat: 0g | Carbohydrates: 40.3g | Fiber: 5.7g | Sugar: 5.3g | Protein: 1.5g

# Strawberry and Beets Sorbet

## Ingredients:

2⅔ cups fresh strawberries, hulled and quartered
⅓ cup cooked beets, quartered

⅓ cup granulated sugar
⅓ cup orange juice

## Preparation:

1. In a high-powered blender, add strawberries and beets and process until smooth. 2. Through a fine-mesh strainer, strain the strawberry puree into a large-sized bowl. 3. Add the sugar and orange juice and stir to combine. 4. Transfer the blended mixture into an empty Ninja CREAMi pint container. 5. Cover the container with storage lid and freeze for 24 hours. 6. After 24 hours, remove the lid from container and arrange into the outer bowl of Ninja CREAMi. 7. Install the "Creamerizer Paddle" onto the lid of outer bowl. 8. Then rotate the lid clockwise to lock. 9. Press "Power" button to turn on the unit. 10. Then press "SORBET" button. 11. When the program is completed, turn the outer bowl and release it from the machine. 12. Transfer the sorbet into serving bowls and enjoy immediately.

Nutritional Information per Serving: Calories: 109 | Fat: 0.4g | Sat Fat: 0g | Carbohydrates: 27.6g | Fiber: 2.2g | Sugar: 24.2g | Protein: 1g

# Fresh Lime Avocado Sorbet

## Ingredients:

¾ cup water
2 tablespoons light corn syrup
Pinch of sea salt

⅔ cup granulated sugar
1 large ripe avocado, peeled, pitted and chopped
3 ounces fresh lime juice

## Preparation:

1. In a medium-sized saucepan, add water, corn syrup and salt and whisk until blended thoroughly. 2. Place the saucepan over medium heat. 3. Slowly add the sugar, beating continuously until blended thoroughly. 4. Bring the mixture to a boil. 5. Remove the saucepan of sugar mixture from heat and set aside to cool completely. 6. In a high-powered blender, add the sugar mixture, avocado and lime juice and process until smooth. 7. Transfer the blended mixture into an empty Ninja CREAMi pint container. 8. Cover the container with storage lid and freeze for 24 hours. 9. After 24 hours, remove the lid from container and arrange into the outer bowl of Ninja CREAMi. 10. Install the "Creamerizer Paddle" onto the lid of outer bowl. 11. Then rotate the lid clockwise to lock. 12. Press "Power" button to turn on the unit. Then press "SORBET" button. 13. When the program is completed, turn the outer bowl and release it from the machine. 14. Transfer the sorbet into serving bowls and enjoy immediately.

Nutritional Information per Serving: Calories: 260 | Fat: 9.8g | Sat Fat: 2.1g | Carbohydrates: 46.7g | Fiber: 3.5g | Sugar: 36.4g | Protein: 1g

# Orange Peach Sorbet

## Ingredients:

1 cup fresh peaches, pitted and sliced
¼ cup orange juice

## Preparation:

1. In a high-powered blender, add peaches and orange juice and process until smooth. 2. Transfer the blended mixture into an empty Ninja CREAMi pint container. 3. Cover the container with storage lid and freeze for 24 hours. 4. After 24 hours, remove the lid from container and arrange into the outer bowl of Ninja CREAMi. 5. Install the "Creamerizer Paddle" onto the lid of outer bowl. 6. Then rotate the lid clockwise to lock. 7. Press "Power" button to turn on the unit. 8. Then press "SORBET" button. 9. When the program is completed, turn the outer bowl and release it from the machine. 10. Transfer the sorbet into serving bowls and enjoy immediately.

Nutritional Information per Serving: Calories: 22 | Fat: 0.1g | Sat Fat: 0.2g | Carbohydrates: 5.1g | Fiber: 0.6g | Sugar: 4.8g | Protein: 0.5g

# Gingered Persimmon Sorbet

## Ingredients:

2½ cups persimmon puree
½ cup sugar
2 teaspoons fresh lemon juice
½ cup water
2 tablespoons crystallized ginger, finely chopped

## Preparation:

1. In a large-sized owl, add persimmon puree, sugar, lemon juice, water and ginger and mix until blended thoroughly. 2. Transfer the blended mixture into an empty Ninja CREAMi pint container. 3. Cover the container with storage lid and freeze for 24 hours. 4. After 24 hours, remove the lid from container and arrange into the outer bowl of Ninja CREAMi. 5. Install the "Creamerizer Paddle" onto the lid of outer bowl. 6. Then rotate the lid clockwise to lock. 7. Press "Power" button to turn on the unit. 8. Then press "SORBET" button. 9. When the program is completed, turn the outer bowl and release it from the machine. 10. Transfer the sorbet into serving bowls and enjoy immediately.

Nutritional Information per Serving: Calories: 366 | Fat: 0.2g | Sat Fat: 0.1g | Carbohydrates: 92.6g | Fiber: 6g | Sugar: 75.8g | Protein: 2.2g

# Refreshing Honeydew Melon Sorbet

## Ingredients:

1 honeydew melon, peeled and cut into 1-inch chunks          2 teaspoons honey
1 tablespoon lemon juice

## Preparation:

1. Arrange the honeydew chunks on a baking sheet and freezer for 4-6 hours. 2. In a high-powered blender, add honeydew chunks, lemon juice and honey and process until smooth. 3. Transfer the blended mixture into an empty Ninja CREAMi pint container. 4. Cover the container with storage lid and freeze for 24 hours. 5. After 24 hours, remove the lid from container and arrange into the outer bowl of Ninja CREAMi. 6. Install the "Creamerizer Paddle" onto the lid of outer bowl. 7. Then rotate the lid clockwise to lock. 8. Press "Power" button to turn on the unit. 9. Then press "SORBET" button. 10. When the program is completed, turn the outer bowl and release it from the machine. 11. Transfer the sorbet into serving bowls and enjoy immediately.

Nutritional Information per Serving: Calories: 127 | Fat: 0.5g | Sat Fat: 0.2g | Carbohydrates: 32.1g | Fiber: 2.6g | Sugar: 28.9g | Protein: 1.8g

# Plum Amaretto Sorbet

## Ingredients:

2 pounds fresh plums, pitted and chopped          2 teaspoons honey
2 tablespoons amaretto

## Preparation:

1. In a high-powered blender, add plums, amaretto and honey and process until smooth. 2. Transfer the blended mixture into an empty Ninja CREAMi pint container. 3. Cover the container with storage lid and freeze for 24 hours. 4. After 24 hours, remove the lid from container and arrange into the outer bowl of Ninja CREAMi. 5. Install the "Creamerizer Paddle" onto the lid of outer bowl. 6. Then rotate the lid clockwise to lock. 7. Press "Power" button to turn on the unit. 8. Then press "SORBET" button. 9. When the program is completed, turn the outer bowl and release it from the machine. 10. Transfer the sorbet into serving bowls and enjoy immediately.

Nutritional Information per Serving: Calories: 48 | Fat: 0.1g | Sat Fat: 0g | Carbohydrates: 6.9g | Fiber: 0.5g | Sugar: 12.4g | Protein: 0.3g

# Lime Apple Pie Sorbet

## Ingredients:

1 (21-ounce can) apple pie filling
¼ cup fresh lime juice

1 teaspoon lime zest

## Preparation:

1. In an empty Ninja CREAMi pint container, place apple pie filling, lime juice and lime zest and stir to blend. 2. Cover the container with storage lid and freeze for 24 hours. 3. After 24 hours, remove the lid from container and arrange into the outer bowl of Ninja CREAMi. 4. Install the "Creamerizer Paddle" onto the lid of outer bowl. 5. Then rotate the lid clockwise to lock. 6. Press "Power" button to turn on the unit. 7. Then press "SORBET" button. 8. When the program is completed, turn the outer bowl and release it from the machine. 9. Transfer the sorbet into serving bowls and enjoy immediately.

**Nutritional Information per Serving:** Calories: 150 | Fat: 0.2g | Sat Fat: 0g | Carbohydrates: 39.1g | Fiber: 1.5g | Sugar: 20.6g | Protein: 0.2g

# Chili Lime Mango Sorbet

## Ingredients:

3 cups frozen mango chunks
½ cup full-fat coconut milk
2 tablespoons maple syrup

2 tablespoons fresh lime juice
1 teaspoon lime zest
1-2 teaspoons chili lime seasoning

## Preparation:

1. In a high-powered blender, add mango chunks and remaining ingredients and process until smooth. 2. Transfer the blended mixture into an empty Ninja CREAMi pint container. 3. Cover the container with storage lid and freeze for 24 hours. 4. After 24 hours, remove the lid from container and arrange into the outer bowl of Ninja CREAMi. 5. Install the "Creamerizer Paddle" onto the lid of outer bowl. 6. Then rotate the lid clockwise to lock. 7. Press "Power" button to turn on the unit. 8. Then press "SORBET" button. 9. When the program is completed, turn the outer bowl and release it from the machine. 10. Transfer the sorbet into serving bowls and enjoy immediately.

**Nutritional Information per Serving:** Calories: 166 | Fat: 6.5g | Sat Fat: 5.6g | Carbohydrates: 27.4g | Fiber: 2g | Sugar: 23.4g | Protein: 1.5g

# Lemon Blueberry Sorbet

## Ingredients:

4 cups frozen blueberries
½ cup water
3 tablespoons honey

3 tablespoons fresh lemon juice
½ teaspoon lemon zest

## Preparation:

1. In a high-powered blender, add blueberries and remaining ingredients and process until smooth. 2. Transfer the blended mixture into an empty Ninja CREAMi pint container. 3. Cover the container with storage lid and freeze for 24 hours. 4. After 24 hours, remove the lid from container and arrange into the outer bowl of Ninja CREAMi. 5. Install the "Creamerizer Paddle" onto the lid of outer bowl. 6. Then rotate the lid clockwise to lock. 7. Press "Power" button to turn on the unit. 8. Then press "SORBET" button. 9. When the program is completed, turn the outer bowl and release it from the machine. 10. Transfer the sorbet into serving bowls and enjoy immediately.

**Nutritional Information per Serving:** Calories: 134 | Fat: 0.6g | Sat Fat: 0.1g | Carbohydrates: 34.3g | Fiber: 3.6g | Sugar: 27.6g | Protein: 1.3g

# Peach, Raspberry & Pineapple Sorbet

## Ingredients:

3 cups peaches, peeled, pitted and sliced
1 cup fresh raspberries
¼ cup pineapple chunks with unsweetened juice

¼ cup fresh orange juice
1 teaspoon honey
½ teaspoon fresh lime juice

## Preparation:

1. In a high-powered blender, add peaches and remaining ingredients and process until smooth. 2. Transfer the blended mixture into an empty Ninja CREAMi pint container. 3. Cover the container with storage lid and freeze for 24 hours. 4. After 24 hours, remove the lid from container and arrange into the outer bowl of Ninja CREAMi. 5. Install the "Creamerizer Paddle" onto the lid of outer bowl. 6. Then rotate the lid clockwise to lock. 7. Press "Power" button to turn on the unit. 8. Then press "SORBET" button. 9. When the program is completed, turn the outer bowl and release it from the machine. 10. Transfer the sorbet into serving bowls and enjoy immediately.

**Nutritional Information per Serving:** Calories: 78 | Fat: 0.5g | Sat Fat: 0g | Carbohydrates: 18.6g | Fiber: 3.9g | Sugar: 15.6g | Protein: 1.6g

# Tropical Fruit Sorbet

## Ingredients:

½ cup sangria seltzer
3 tablespoons raw agave nectar

1 (15¼-ounce) can tropical fruit in a heavy syrup, drained

## Preparation:

1. In a large-sized bowl, add the seltzer and agave nectar and whisk blended thoroughly. 2. In an empty Ninja CREAMi pint container, place the fruit and top with agave mixture. 3. Cover the container with storage lid and freeze for 24 hours. 4. After 24 hours, remove the lid from container and arrange into the outer bowl of Ninja CREAMi. 5. Install the "Creamerizer Paddle" onto the lid of outer bowl. 6. Then rotate the lid clockwise to lock. 7. Press "Power" button to turn on the unit. 8. Then press "SORBET" button. 9. When the program is completed, turn the outer bowl and release it from the machine. 10. Transfer the sorbet into serving bowls and enjoy immediately.

**Nutritional Information per Serving:** Calories: 135 | Fat: 0g | Sat Fat: 0g | Carbohydrates: 32.4g | Fiber: 1.1g | Sugar: 25.2g | Protein: 0.3g

# Refreshing Citrus Mojito Sorbet

## Ingredients:

½ cup water
½ cup white sugar
¼ cup mint leaves, packed
1 teaspoon grated lime zest

½ cup freshly squeezed lime juice
¾ cup citrus-flavored sparkling water
1 tablespoon rum (optional)

## Preparation:

1. Combine all ingredients in a bowl and mix until the sugar dissolves. Pour the mixture into the Ninja CREAMi Pint container and freeze it on a flat surface in a cold freezer for 24 hours. 2. After 24 hours, take the Pint out of the freezer and remove the lid. 3. Place the Ninja CREAMi Pint into the outer bowl. Insert the outer bowl with the Pint into the Ninja CREAMi machine and twist until it locks. Press the SORBET button. The mixture will blend and become creamy, which should take about 2 minutes. 4. When the SORBET function finishes, turn the outer bowl and remove it from the Ninja CREAMi machine. 5. Your sorbet is ready to enjoy!

**Nutritional Information per Serving:** Calories 56 | Protein 0.1g | Carbohydrate 14g | Dietary Fiber 0.2g | Sugar 12g | Fat 0.1g | Sodium 1.6mg

# Pineapple Rum Sorbet

## Ingredients:

¾ cup piña colada mix

¼ cup rum

2 tablespoons granulated sugar

1½ cups frozen pineapple chunks

## Preparation:

1. In a high-speed blender, add all the ingredients and pulse until smooth. 2. Transfer the mixture into an empty Ninja CREAMi pint container. 3. Cover the container with storage lid and freeze for 24 hours. 4. After 24 hours, remove the lid from container and arrange into the Outer Bowl of Ninja CREAMi. 5. Install the Creamerizer Paddle onto the lid of Outer Bowl. 6. Then rotate the lid clockwise to lock. 7. Press Power button to turn on the unit. 8. Then press Sorbet button. 9. When the program is completed, turn the Outer Bowl and release it from the machine. 10. Transfer the sorbet into serving bowls and serve immediately.

**Nutritional Information per Serving:** Calories: 102 | Fat: 0.2g | Sat Fat: 0g | Carbohydrates: 17.6g | Fiber: 1.8g | Sugar: 14.4g | Protein: 0.6g

# Lemon Pineapple Sorbet

## Ingredients:

16 ounces canned pineapple chunks, with juice

1 teaspoon lemon juice

1 teaspoon lemon zest

1 small piece of ginger, sliced

1 teaspoon basil leaves

⅓ cup white caster sugar

## Preparation:

1. Place all the ingredients in a blender. Mix well until smooth. 2. Pour the mixture into the Ninja CREAMi Pint and close the lid. 3. Place the pint into the freezer and freeze for 24 hours. 4. Once done, open the lid, place the pint into the outer bowl of the Ninja CREAMi, and set the Creamerizer Paddle into the outer bowl. 5. Lock the lid by rotating it clockwise. 6. Turn the unit on and press the SORBET button. 7. Once done, take out the bowl from the Ninja CREAMi. 8. Serve and enjoy this yummy sorbet.

**Nutritional Information per Serving:** Calories: 34 | Fat: 0.1g | Sat Fat: 0g | Carbohydrates: 8.9g | Fiber: 0.5g | Sugar: 5.9g | Protein: 0.1g

# Watermelon Sorbet

## Ingredients:

3½ cups seedless watermelon chunks

2 teaspoons lime juice

¼ cup warm water

## Preparation:

1. Place all the ingredients in a blender. Mix well until smooth. 2. Pour the mixture into the Ninja CREAMi Pint and close the lid. 3. Place the pint into the freezer and freeze for 24 hours. 4. Once done, open the lid and place the pint into the outer bowl of the Ninja CREAMi. Set the Creamerizer Paddle into the outer bowl. 5. Lock the lid by rotating it clockwise. 6. Turn on the unit and press the SORBET button. 7. Once done, take out the bowl from the Ninja CREAMi. 8. Serve and enjoy your yummy sorbet.

**Nutritional Information per Serving:** Calories: 177 | Fat: 0.8g | Sat Fat: 0.4g | Carbohydrates: 44.3g | Fiber: 2.3g | Sugar: 36.2g | Protein: 3.5g

# Sweet Lemon Rhubarb Sorbet

## Ingredients:

3 cups rhubarb, chopped

½ teaspoon vanilla extract

⅔ cup golden caster sugar

3 tablespoons liquid glucose

2 teaspoons star anise

1 cup lemon juice

## Preparation:

1. Add the ingredients to a blender. Mix well until smooth. 2. Pour the mixture into the Ninja CREAMi Pint and close the lid. 3. Place the pint into the freezer and freeze for 24 hours. 4. Once done, open the lid and place the pint into the outer bowl of the Ninja CREAMi. Set the Creamerizer Paddle into the outer bowl. 5. Lock the lid by rotating it clockwise. 6. Turn the unit on and press the SORBET button. 7. Once done, take out the bowl from the Ninja CREAMi. 8. Serve and enjoy this yummy sorbet.

**Nutritional Information per Serving:** Calories: 17 | Fat: 0.2g | Sat Fat: 0g | Carbohydrates: 3.6g | Fiber: 1.2g | Sugar: 1.1g | Protein: 0.7g

# Chapter 6 Gelato

# Vanilla Bean Gelato

## Ingredients:

4 large egg yolks
1 tablespoon light corn syrup
¼ cup plus 1 tablespoon granulated sugar

1 cup heavy cream
⅓ cup whole milk
1 whole vanilla bean, split in half lengthwise and scraped

## Preparation:

1. In a small-sized saucepan, add the egg yolks, corn syrup and sugar and whisk until blended thoroughly. 2. Add the heavy cream, milk and vanilla bean and whisk until blended thoroughly. 3. Cook for about 2-3 minutes over medium heat and, stirring continuously. 4. Remove the saucepan of milk mixture from heat and through a fine-mesh strainer, strain the mixture into an empty Ninja CREAMi pint container. 5. Place the container into an ice bath to cool. 6. After cooling, cover the container with the storage lid and freeze for 24 hours. 7. After 24 hours, remove the lid from container and arrange into the outer bowl of Ninja CREAMi. 8. Install the "Creamerizer Paddle" onto the lid of outer bowl. 9. Then rotate the lid clockwise to lock. 10. Press "Power" button to turn on the unit. 11. Then press "GELATO" button. 12. When the program is completed, turn the outer bowl and release it from the machine. 13. Transfer the gelato into serving bowls and serve immediately.

**Nutritional Information per Serving:** Calories: 239 | Fat: 16.3g | Sat Fat: 3.1g | Carbohydrates: 21g | Fiber: 0g | Sugar: 17.5g | Protein: 4g

# Classic Chocolate Hazelnut Gelato

## Ingredients:

3 large egg yolks
⅓ cup hazelnut spread
¼ cup granulated sugar
2 teaspoons cocoa powder

1 tablespoon light corn syrup
1 cup whole milk
½ cup heavy cream
1 teaspoon vanilla extract

## Preparation:

1. In a small-sized saucepan, add the egg yolks, hazelnut spread, sugar, cocoa powder and corn syrup and whisk until blended thoroughly. 2. Add the milk, heavy cream and vanilla extract and whisk until blended thoroughly. 3. Place the saucepan over medium heat and cook for about 2-3 minutes, stirring continuously. 4. Remove the pan of milk mixture from heat and through a fine-mesh strainer, strain the mixture into an empty Ninja CREAMi pint container. 5. Place the container into an ice bath to cool. 6. After cooling, cover the container with the storage lid and freeze for 24 hours. 7. After 24 hours, remove the lid from container and arrange into the outer bowl of Ninja CREAMi. 8. Install the "Creamerizer Paddle" onto the lid of outer bowl. 9. Then rotate the lid clockwise to lock. 10. Press "Power" button to turn on the unit. 11. Then press "GELATO" button. 12. When the program is completed, turn the outer bowl and release it from the machine. 13. Transfer the gelato into serving bowls and serve immediately.

**Nutritional Information per Serving:** Calories: 321 | Fat: 19g | Sat Fat: 2.9g | Carbohydrates: 33.7g | Fiber: 0.9g | Sugar: 22.9g | Protein: 5.9g

# Delicious Caramel Gelato

Preparation Time: 10 minutes | Cooking Time: 10 minutes | Servings: 4

## Ingredients:

¼ cup agave nectar
¾ cup unsweetened soy milk
½ cup unsweetened creamer

2 eggs
3 tablespoons granulated sugar
¼ cup caramels, chopped

## Preparation:

1. In a medium-sized saucepan, add agave nectar over medium-high heat and cook for about 2-3 minutes. 2. Remove the saucepan from heat and slowly whisk in the soy milk and creamer. 3. Return the pan over medium-high heat and whisk in the eggs and sugar. 4. Cook for about 4-5 minutes, stirring frequently. 5. Remove the saucepan of milk mixture from heat and through a fine-mesh strainer, strain the mixture into an empty Ninja CREAMi pint container. 6. Place the container into an ice bath to cool. 7. After cooling, cover the container with the storage lid and freeze for 24 hours. 8. After 24 hours, remove the lid from container and arrange into the outer bowl of Ninja CREAMi. 9. Install the "Creamerizer Paddle" onto the lid of outer bowl. 10. Then rotate the lid clockwise to lock. 11. Press "Power" button to turn on the unit. 12. Then press "GELATO" button. 13. When the program is completed, with a spoon, create a 1½-inch wide hole in the center that reaches the bottom of the pint container. 14. Add the chopped caramels into the hole and press "MIX-IN" button. 15. When the program is completed, turn the outer bowl and release it from the machine. 16. Transfer the gelato into serving bowls and serve immediately.

**Nutritional Information per Serving:** Calories: 174 | Fat: 4.8g | Sat Fat: 1.1g | Carbohydrates: 29.8g | Fiber: 1.3g | Sugar: 27.1g | Protein: 4.6g

# Healthy Pecan Gelato

Preparation Time: 10 minutes | Cooking Time: 3 minutes | Servings: 4

## Ingredients:

4 large egg yolks
5 tablespoons granulated sugar
1 tablespoon light corn syrup
1 cup heavy cream

⅓ cup whole milk
1 teaspoon butter flavor extract
⅓ cup pecans, chopped

## Preparation:

1. In a small-sized saucepan, add the egg yolks, sugar and corn syrup and whisk until blended thoroughly. 2. Add the heavy cream, milk and butter flavor extract and whisk until blended thoroughly. 3. Place the saucepan over medium heat and cook for about 2-3 minutes, stirring continuously. 4. Remove the saucepan of milk mixture from heat and through a fine-mesh strainer, strain the mixture into an empty Ninja CREAMi pint container. 5. Place the container into an ice bath to cool. 6. After cooling, cover the container with the storage lid and freeze for 24 hours. 7. After 24 hours, remove the lid from container and arrange into the outer bowl of Ninja CREAMi. 8. Install the "Creamerizer Paddle" onto the lid of outer bowl. 9. Then rotate the lid clockwise to lock. 10. Press "Power" button to turn on the unit. 11. Then press "GELATO" button. 12. When the program is completed, with a spoon, create a 1½-inch wide hole in the center that reaches the bottom of the pint container. 13. Add the pecans into the hole and press "MIX-IN" button. 14. When the program is completed, turn the outer bowl and release it from the machine. 15. Transfer the gelato into serving bowls and serve immediately.

**Nutritional Information per Serving:** Calories: 319 | Fat: 24.5g | Sat Fat: 5.2g | Carbohydrates: 22.6g | Fiber: 1.2g | Sugar: 17.8g | Protein: 5.2g

# Red Velvet Cocoa Gelato

## Ingredients:

4 large egg yolks
¼ cup granulated sugar
2 tablespoons unsweetened cocoa powder
1 cup whole milk

⅓ cup heavy whipping cream
¼ cup cream cheese, softened
1 teaspoon vanilla extract
1 teaspoon red food coloring

## Preparation:

1. In a small-sized saucepan, add the egg yolks, sugar and cocoa powder and whisk until blended thoroughly. 2. Add the milk, heavy cream, cream cheese, vanilla extract and food coloring and whisk until blended thoroughly. 3. Place the saucepan over medium heat and cook for about 2-3 minutes, stirring continuously. 4. Remove the saucepan of milk mixture from heat and through a fine-mesh strainer, strain the mixture into an empty Ninja CREAMi pint container. 5. Place the container into an ice bath to cool. 6. After cooling, cover the container with the storage lid and freeze for 24 hours. 7. After 24 hours, remove the lid from container and arrange into the outer bowl of Ninja CREAMi. 8. Install the "Creamerizer Paddle" onto the lid of outer bowl. 9. Then rotate the lid clockwise to lock. 10. Press "Power" button to turn on the unit. 11. Then press "GELATO" button. 12. When the program is completed, turn the outer bowl and release it from the machine. 13. Transfer the gelato into serving bowls and serve immediately.

**Nutritional Information per Serving:** Calories: 232 | Fat: 15.6g | Sat Fat: 4.5g | Carbohydrates: 18.1g | Fiber: 0.9g | Sugar: 16g | Protein: 6.5g

# Chocolate Gelato

## Ingredients:

4 large egg yolks
⅓ cup dark brown sugar
1 tablespoon dark cocoa powder
1 tablespoon chocolate fudge topping

¾ cup heavy cream
¾ cup whole milk
2-3 tablespoons chocolate chunks, chopped

## Preparation:

1. In a small-sized saucepan, add the egg yolks, sugar, cocoa powder and chocolate fudge and whisk until blended thoroughly. 2. Add the heavy cream and milk and whisk until blended thoroughly. 3. Place the saucepan over medium heat and cook for about 2-3 minutes, stirring continuously. 4. Remove the saucepan of milk mixture from heat and stir in chocolate chunks until melted completely. 5. Through a fine-mesh strainer, strain the mixture into an empty Ninja CREAMi pint container. 6. Place the container into an ice bath to cool. 7. After cooling, cover the container with the storage lid and freeze for 24 hours. 8. After 24 hours, remove the lid from container and arrange into the outer bowl of Ninja CREAMi. 9. Install the "Creamerizer Paddle" onto the lid of outer bowl. 10. Then rotate the lid clockwise to lock. 11. Press "Power" button to turn on the unit. 12. Then press "GELATO" button. 13. When the program is completed, turn the outer bowl and release it from the machine. 14. Transfer the gelato into serving bowls and serve immediately.

**Nutritional Information per Serving:** Calories: 256 | Fat: 16.7g | Sat Fat: 4.5g | Carbohydrates: 22.8g | Fiber: 1.1g | Sugar: 18.7g | Protein: 5.8g

# Blueberry Gelato with Graham Crackers

## Ingredients:

4 large egg yolks
3 tablespoons granulated sugar
3 tablespoons wild blueberry preserves
1 teaspoon vanilla extract
1 cup whole milk

⅓ cup heavy cream
¼ cup cream cheese, softened
3-6 drops purple food coloring
2 large graham crackers, broken in 1-inch pieces

## Preparation:

1. In a small-sized saucepan, add the egg yolks, sugar, blueberry preserves and vanilla extract and whisk until blended thoroughly. 2. Add the milk, heavy cream, cream cheese and food coloring and whisk until blended thoroughly. 3. Place the saucepan over medium heat and cook for about 2-3 minutes, stirring continuously. 4. Remove the saucepan of milk mixture from heat and through a fine-mesh strainer, strain the mixture into an empty Ninja CREAMi pint container. 5. Place the container into an ice bath to cool. 6. After cooling, cover the container with the storage lid and freeze for 24 hours. 7. After 24 hours, remove the lid from container and arrange into the outer bowl of Ninja CREAMi. 8. Install the "Creamerizer Paddle" onto the lid of outer bowl. 9. Then rotate the lid clockwise to lock. 10. Press "Power" button to turn on the unit. 11. Then press "GELATO" button. 12. When the program is completed, with a spoon, create a 1½-inch wide hole in the center that reaches the bottom of the pint container. 13. Add the graham crackers into the hole and press "MIX-IN" button. 14. When the program is completed, turn the outer bowl and release it from the machine. 15. Transfer the gelato into serving bowls and serve immediately.

Nutritional Information per Serving: Calories: 279 | Fat: 16g | Sat Fat: 2.1g | Carbohydrates: 28.3g | Fiber: 0.2g | Sugar: 23.7g | Protein: 6.4g

# Chocolate Peanut Butter Gelato

## Ingredients:

1½ cups unsweetened coconut milk
6 tablespoons sugar
1 tablespoon cornstarch

3 tablespoons peanut butter
3 dark chocolate peanut butter cups, cut each into 8 pieces
2 tablespoons peanuts, chopped

## Preparation:

1. In a small-sized saucepan, add the coconut milk, sugar, and cornstarch and mix well. 2. Place the saucepan over medium heat and bring to a boil, whisking continuously. 3. Now, adjust the heat to low and simmer for about 3-4 minutes. 4. Remove the pan of milk mixture from heat and stir in the peanut butter. 5. Transfer the mixture into an empty Ninja CREAMi pint container. 6. Place the container into an ice bath to cool. 7. After cooling, cover the container with the storage lid and freeze for 24 hours. 8. After 24 hours, remove the lid from container and arrange into the outer bowl of Ninja CREAMi. 9. Install the "Creamerizer Paddle" onto the lid of outer bowl. 10. Then rotate the lid clockwise to lock. 11. Press "Power" button to turn on the unit. 12. Then press "GELATO" button. 13. When the program is completed, with a spoon, create a 1½-inch wide hole in the center that reaches the bottom of the pint container. 14. Add the peanut butter cup pieces and peanuts into the hole and press "MIX-IN" button. 15. When the program is completed, turn the outer bowl and release it from the machine. 16. Transfer the gelato into serving bowls and serve immediately.

Nutritional Information per Serving: Calories: 426 | Fat: 29.7g | Sat Fat: 17.3g | Carbohydrates: 34.2g | Fiber: 1.1g | Sugar: 29.1g | Protein: 6.8g

# Black Cherry Gelato

## Ingredients:

4 large egg yolks

1 tablespoon light corn syrup

5 tablespoons granulated sugar

1 cup heavy cream

⅓ cup whole milk

1 teaspoon almond extract

1 cup frozen black cherries, pitted and quartered

## Preparation:

1. In a small-sized saucepan, add the egg yolks, sugar and corn syrup and whisk until blended thoroughly. 2. Add the heavy cream, milk and almond extract and whisk until blended thoroughly. 3. Place the saucepan over medium heat and cook for about 2-3 minutes, stirring continuously. 4. Remove the pan of milk mixture from heat and through a fine-mesh strainer, strain the mixture into an empty Ninja CREAMi pint container. 5. Place the container into an ice bath to cool. 6. After cooling, cover the container with the storage lid and freeze for 24 hours. 7. After 24 hours, remove the lid from container and arrange into the outer bowl of Ninja CREAMi. 8. Install the "Creamerizer Paddle" onto the lid of outer bowl. 9. Then rotate the lid clockwise to lock. 10. Press "Power" button to turn on the unit. 11. Then press "GELATO" button. 12. When the program is completed, with a spoon, create a 1½-inch wide hole in the center that reaches the bottom of the pint container. 13. Add the cherries into the hole and press "MIX-IN" button. 14. When the program is completed, turn the outer bowl and release it from the machine. 15. Transfer the gelato into serving bowls and serve immediately.

**Nutritional Information per Serving:** Calories: 260 | Fat: 16.4g | Sat Fat: 3.7g | Carbohydrates: 25.4g | Fiber: 0.6g | Sugar: 21.1g | Protein: 4.3g

# Vanilla Pumpkin Gelato

## Ingredients:

3 large egg yolks

⅓ cup granulated sugar

1 tablespoon maple syrup

1 cup whole milk

½ cup heavy cream

½ cup canned pumpkin puree

1½ teaspoons pumpkin pie spice

1 teaspoon vanilla extract

## Preparation:

1. In a small-sized saucepan, add the egg yolks, sugar and maple syrup and whisk until blended thoroughly. 2. Add the milk, heavy cream, pumpkin puree and pumpkin pie spice and whisk until blended thoroughly. 3. Place the saucepan over medium heat and cook for about 2-3 minutes, stirring continuously. 4. Remove the pan of milk mixture from heat and stir in the vanilla extract. 5. Through a fine-mesh strainer, strain the mixture into an empty Ninja CREAMi pint container. 6. Place the container into an ice bath to cool. 7. After cooling, cover the container with the storage lid and freeze for 24 hours. 8. After 24 hours, remove the lid from container and arrange into the outer bowl of Ninja CREAMi. 9. Install the "Creamerizer Paddle" onto the lid of outer bowl. 10. Then rotate the lid clockwise to lock. 11. Press "Power" button to turn on the unit. 12. Then press "GELATO" button. 13. When the program is completed, turn the outer bowl and release it from the machine. 14. Transfer the gelato into serving bowls and serve immediately.

**Nutritional Information per Serving:** Calories: 220 | Fat: 11.1g | Sat Fat: 3.1g | Carbohydrates: 21g | Fiber: 1g | Sugar: 22.4g | Protein: 4.7g

# Dark Chocolate & Cauliflower Gelato

## Ingredients:

1 cup whole milk
½ cup heavy cream
⅓ cup sugar
2 tablespoon cocoa powder

½ cup frozen cauliflower rice
¼ teaspoon almond extract
Pinch of salt
½ cup dark chocolate, chopped

## Preparation:

1. In a small-sized saucepan, add milk and remaining ingredients except for chopped chocolate and whisk until blended thoroughly. 2. Place the saucepan over medium heat and cook for about 2-3 minutes, stirring continuously. 3. Remove the saucepan of milk mixture from heat and transfer the mixture into an empty Ninja CREAMi pint container. 4. Place the container into an ice bath to cool. 5. After cooling, cover the container with the storage lid and freeze for 24 hours. 6. After 24 hours, remove the lid from container and arrange into the outer bowl of Ninja CREAMi. 7. Install the "Creamerizer Paddle" onto the lid of outer bowl. 8. Then rotate the lid clockwise to lock. 9. Press "Power" button to turn on the unit. 10. Then press "GELATO" button. 11. When the program is completed, with a spoon, create a 1½-inch wide hole in the center that reaches the bottom of the pint container. 12. Add the chopped chocolate into the hole and press "MIX-IN" button. 13. When the program is completed, turn the outer bowl and release it from the machine. 14. Transfer the gelato into serving bowls and serve immediately.

**Nutritional Information per Serving:** Calories: 273 | Fat: 14.1g | Sat Fat: 3.9g | Carbohydrates: 34.5g | Fiber: 1.8g | Sugar: 31.1g | Protein: 4.6g

# Delicious Maple Gelato

## Ingredients:

4 large egg yolks
½ cup plus 1 tablespoon light brown sugar
1 tablespoon maple syrup

1 teaspoon maple extract
1 cup whole milk
⅓ cup heavy cream

## Preparation:

1. In a small-sized saucepan, add the egg yolks, brown sugar, maple syrup and maple extract and whisk until blended thoroughly. 2. Add the milk and heavy cream and whisk until blended thoroughly. 3. Place the saucepan of milk mixture over medium heat and cook for about 2-3 minutes, stirring continuously. 4. Remove the saucepan of milk mixture from heat and through a fine-mesh strainer, strain the mixture into an empty Ninja CREAMi pint container. 5. Place the container into an ice bath to cool. 6. After cooling, cover the container with the storage lid and freeze for 24 hours. 7. After 24 hours, remove the lid from container and arrange into the outer bowl of Ninja CREAMi. 8. Install the "Creamerizer Paddle" onto the lid of outer bowl. 9. Then rotate the lid clockwise to lock. 10. Press "Power" button to turn on the unit. 11. Then press "GELATO" button. 12. When the program is completed, turn the outer bowl and release it from the machine. 13. Transfer the gelato into serving bowls and serve immediately.

**Nutritional Information per Serving:** Calories: 218 | Fat: 10.2g | Sat Fat: 3.1g | Carbohydrates: 27g | Fiber: 0g | Sugar: 26.1g | Protein: 4.9g

# Cinnamon Sweet Potato Gelato

Preparation Time: 10 minutes | Cooking Time: 3 minutes | Servings: 4

## Ingredients:

½ cup canned sweet potato puree
4 large egg yolks
¼ cup sugar
½ teaspoon ground cinnamon

⅛ teaspoon ground nutmeg
Pinch of ground cloves
1 cup heavy cream
1 teaspoon vanilla extract

## Preparation:

1. In a small-sized saucepan, add the sweet potato puree, egg yolks, sugar, ground cloves, ½ teaspoon of cinnamon and nutmeg and whisk until blended thoroughly. 2. Add the heavy cream and vanilla extract and whisk until blended thoroughly. 3. Place the saucepan over medium heat and cook for about 2-3 minutes, stirring continuously. 4. Remove the pan of cream mixture from heat and through a fine-mesh strainer, strain the mixture into an empty Ninja CREAMi pint container. 5. Place the container into an ice bath to cool. 6. After cooling, cover the container with the storage lid and freeze for 24 hours. 7. After 24 hours, remove the lid from container and arrange into the outer bowl of Ninja CREAMi. 8. Install the "Creamerizer Paddle" onto the lid of outer bowl. 9. Then rotate the lid clockwise to lock. 10. Press "Power" button to turn on the unit. 11. Then press "GELATO" button. 12. When the program is completed, turn the outer bowl and release it from the machine. 13. Transfer the gelato into serving bowls and serve immediately.

**Nutritional Information per Serving:** Calories: 239 | Fat: 15.7g | Sat Fat: 5.1g | Carbohydrates: 21.5g | Fiber: 0.9g | Sugar: 14g | Protein: 4g

# Honey Beet Gelato

Preparation Time: 10 minutes | Cooking Time: 3 minutes | Servings: 4

## Ingredients:

3 large egg yolks
⅓ cup sugar
1 tablespoon honey
½ cup heavy cream

1 cup milk
½ cup beet puree
1 teaspoon ground cinnamon
1 teaspoon vanilla extract

## Preparation:

1. In a small-sized saucepan, add the egg yolks, sugar and honey and whisk until blended thoroughly. 2. Add the heavy cream, milk, beet puree and cinnamon and whisk until blended thoroughly. 3. Place the saucepan over medium heat and cook for about 2-3 minutes, stirring continuously. 4. Remove the pan of milk mixture from heat and stir in the vanilla extract. 5. Through a fine-mesh strainer, strain the mixture into an empty Ninja CREAMi pint container. 6. Place the container into an ice bath to cool. 7. After cooling, cover the container with the storage lid and freeze for 24 hours. 8. After 24 hours, remove the lid from container and arrange into the outer bowl of Ninja CREAMi. 9. Install the "Creamerizer Paddle" onto the lid of outer bowl. 10. Then rotate the lid clockwise to lock. 11. Press "Power" button to turn on the unit. 12. Then press "GELATO" button. 13. When the program is completed, turn the outer bowl and release it from the machine. 14. Transfer the gelato into serving bowls and serve immediately.

**Nutritional Information per Serving:** Calories: 215 | Fat: 10.2g | Sat Fat: 5.4g | Carbohydrates: 27.6g | Fiber: 0.8g | Sugar: 25.7g | Protein: 4.7g

# Tasty Coffee Gelato

## Ingredients:

⅓ cup granulated sugar
1 cup whole milk
¾ cup heavy cream

2 egg yolks
1½ tablespoons instant coffee
1 teaspoon vanilla extract

## Preparation:

1. In a small-sized saucepan, add the egg yolks and sugar and whisk until blended thoroughly. 2. Add the heavy cream, milk, coffee and vanilla extract and whisk until blended thoroughly. 3. Place the saucepan over medium heat and cook for about 4-5 minutes, stirring continuously. 4. Remove the pan of milk mixture from heat and stir in the vanilla extract. 5. Through a fine-mesh strainer, strain the mixture into an empty Ninja CREAMi pint container. 6. Place the container into an ice bath to cool. 7. After cooling, cover the container with the storage lid and freeze for 24 hours. 8. After 24 hours, remove the lid from container and arrange into the outer bowl of Ninja CREAMi. 9. Install the "Creamerizer Paddle" onto the lid of outer bowl. 10. Then rotate the lid clockwise to lock. 11. Press "Power" button to turn on the unit. 12. Then press "GELATO" button. 13. When the program is completed, turn the outer bowl and release it from the machine. 14. Transfer the gelato into serving bowls and serve immediately.

Nutritional Information per Serving: Calories: 207 | Fat: 12.6g | Sat Fat: 7.1g | Carbohydrates: 20.5g | Fiber: 0g | Sugar: 20.1g | Protein: 3.8g

# Raspberry Gelato

## Ingredients:

4 large egg yolks
1 tablespoon maple syrup
5 tablespoons white sugar
1 cup heavy cream

⅓ cup whole milk
1 teaspoon vanilla extract
1 cup frozen raspberries, halved

## Preparation:

1. In a small-sized saucepan, put egg yolks, maple syrup and white sugar and whisk to incorporate thoroughly. 2. Add the heavy cream, milk and vanilla extract and whisk to incorporate thoroughly. 3. Place the saucepan on burner at around medium heat and cook for around 2-3 minutes, stirring continuously. 4. Take off the pan of milk mixture from burner and through a fine-mesh strainer, strain the mixture into an empty Ninja CREAMi pint container. 5. Place the container into an ice bath to cool. 6. After cooling, cover the container with the storage lid and freeze for 24 hours. 7. After 24 hours, take off the lid from container and arrange into the outer bowl of Ninja CREAMi. 8. Install the "Creamerizer Paddle" onto the lid of outer bowl. 9. Then rotate the lid clockwise to lock. 10. Press "Power" button to turn on the unit. 11. Then press "GELATO" button. 12. When the program is completed, with a spoon, create a 1½-inch wide hole in the center that reaches the bottom of the pint container. 13. Add the raspberries into the hole and press "MIX-IN" button. 14. When the program is completed, turn the outer bowl and release it from the machine. 15. Transfer the gelato into serving bowls and serve immediately.

Nutritional Information per Serving: Calories: 256 | Fat: 16.1g | Sat Fat: 3.4g | Carbohydrates: 22.4g | Fiber: 0.4g | Sugar: 19.1g | Protein: 4.1g

# Spirulina Gelato with Chocolate Chip Cookies

## Ingredients:

4 large egg yolks

⅓ cup granulated sugar

1 cup oat milk

1 teaspoon vanilla extract

1 teaspoon blue spirulina powder

4 small crunchy chocolate chip cookies, crumbled

## Preparation:

1. In a small-sized saucepan, add the egg yolks and sugar and whisk until blended thoroughly. 2. Add oat milk, vanilla extract and blue spirulina powder and stir to combine. 3. Place the saucepan over medium heat and cook for about 2-3 minutes, stirring continuously. 4. Remove the saucepan of milk mixture from heat and through a fine-mesh strainer, strain the mixture into an empty Ninja CREAMi pint container. 5. Place the container into an ice bath to cool. 6. After cooling, cover the container with the storage lid and freeze for 24 hours. 7. After 24 hours, remove the lid from container and arrange into the outer bowl of Ninja CREAMi. 8. Install the "Creamerizer Paddle" onto the lid of outer bowl. 9. Then rotate the lid clockwise to lock. 10. Press "Power" button to turn on the unit. 11. Then press "GELATO" button. 12. When the program is completed, with a spoon, create a 1½-inch wide hole in the center that reaches the bottom of the pint container. 13. Add the chocolate chip cookies into the hole and press "MIX-IN" button. 14. When the program is completed, turn the outer bowl and release it from the machine. 15. Transfer the gelato into serving bowls and serve immediately.

Nutritional Information per Serving: Calories: 235 | Fat: 8.9g | Sat Fat: 1.1g | Carbohydrates: 35.4g | Fiber: 0.5g | Sugar: 21.7g | Protein: 4.5g

# Mixed Berries Cheese Gelato

## Ingredients:

3 large egg yolks
½ cup plus 2 tablespoons granulated sugar, divided
1 tablespoon light corn syrup
½ cup mascarpone

¾ cup whole milk
¼ cup heavy cream
½ teaspoon vanilla extract
1 cup frozen mixed berries

## Preparation:

1. In a small-sized saucepan, add the egg yolks, ½ cup of sugar and corn syrup and whisk until blended thoroughly. 2. Add the mascarpone, milk, heavy cream and vanilla extract and whisk until blended thoroughly. 3. Place the saucepan over medium heat and cook for about 2-3 minutes, stirring continuously. 4. Remove the saucepan of milk mixture from heat and through a fine-mesh strainer, strain the mixture into an empty Ninja CREAMi pint container. 5. Place the container into an ice bath to cool. 6. After cooling, cover the container with the storage lid and freeze for 24 hours. 7. Meanwhile, in a small-sized saucepan, add the mixed berries and remaining sugar over medium heat and cook for about 8 minutes, stirring occasionally and mashing to form a thick jam. 8. Remove the saucepan of berry mixture from heat and transfer the jam into a bowl. 9. Refrigerate the frozen mixed berries until using. 10. After 24 hours, remove the lid from container and arrange the container into the outer bowl of Ninja CREAMi. 11. Install the "Creamerizer Paddle" onto the lid of outer bowl. 12. Then rotate the lid clockwise to lock. 13. Press "Power" button to turn on the unit. 14. Then press "GELATO" button. 15. When the program is completed, with a spoon, create a 1½-inch wide hole in the center that reaches the bottom of the pint container. 16. Add the mixed berries into the hole and press "MIX-IN" button. 17. When the program is completed, turn the outer bowl and release it from the machine. 18. Transfer the gelato into serving bowls and serve immediately.

Nutritional Information per Serving: Calories: 295 | Fat: 11.8g | Sat Fat: 2.9g | Carbohydrates: 41.6g | Fiber: 1.3g | Sugar: 36.4g | Protein: 7.4g

# Spiced Carrot Gelato

## Ingredients:

3 large egg yolks
⅓ cup coconut sugar
1 tablespoon brown rice syrup
½ cup heavy cream
1 cup unsweetened almond milk
½ cup carrot puree

½ teaspoon ground cinnamon
¼ teaspoon ground nutmeg
¼ teaspoon ground ginger
¼ teaspoon ground cloves
¾ teaspoon vanilla extract

## Preparation:

1. In a small-sized saucepan, add the egg yolks, coconut sugar and brown rice syrup and whisk until blended thoroughly. 2. Add the heavy cream, almond milk, carrot puree and spices and whisk until blended thoroughly. 3. Place the saucepan over medium heat and cook for about 2-3 minutes, stirring continuously. 4. Remove the pan of milk mixture from heat and stir in the vanilla extract. 5. Through a fine-mesh strainer, strain the mixture into an empty Ninja CREAMi pint container. 6. Place the container into an ice bath to cool. 7. After cooling, cover the container with the storage lid and freeze for 24 hours. 8. After cooling, cover the container with the storage lid and freeze for 24 hours. 9. After 24 hours, remove the lid from container and arrange into the outer bowl of Ninja CREAMi. 10. Install the "Creamerizer Paddle" onto the lid of outer bowl. 11. Then rotate the lid clockwise to lock. 12. Press "Power" button to turn on the unit. 13. Then press "GELATO" button. 14. When the program is completed, turn the outer bowl and release it from the machine. 15. Transfer the gelato into serving bowls and serve immediately.

**Nutritional Information per Serving:** Calories: 146 | Fat: 6.5g | Sat Fat: 0.9g | Carbohydrates: 22.7g | Fiber: 0.8g | Sugar: 20g | Protein: 0.8g

# Butternut Squash & Banana Gelato

## Ingredients:

4 large egg yolks
1 cup heavy cream
⅓ cup granulated sugar
½ of banana, peeled and sliced

½ cup frozen butternut squash, chopped
1 (3½-ounce) box instant vanilla pudding mix
6 vanilla wafer cookies, crumbled

## Preparation:

1. In a small-sized saucepan, add the egg yolks, heavy cream and sugar and whisk until blended thoroughly. 2. Place the saucepan over medium heat and cook for about 2-3 minutes, stirring continuously. 3. Remove the saucepan of egg mixture from heat and through a fine-mesh strainer, strain the mixture into an empty Ninja CREAMi pint container. 4. Place the container into an ice bath to cool. 5. After cooling, add in the banana, squash and pudding until blended thoroughly. 6. Cover the container with the storage lid and freeze for 24 hours. 7. After 24 hours, remove the lid from container and arrange into the outer bowl of Ninja CREAMi. 8. Install the "Creamerizer Paddle" onto the lid of outer bowl. 9. Then rotate the lid clockwise to lock. 10. Press "Power" button to turn on the unit. 11. Then press "GELATO" button. 12. When the program is completed, with a spoon, create a 1½-inch wide hole in the center that reaches the bottom of the pint container. 13. Add the wafer cookies into the hole and press "MIX-IN" button. 14. When the program is completed, turn the outer bowl and release it from the machine. 15. Transfer the gelato into serving bowls and serve immediately.

Nutritional Information per Serving: Calories: 296 | Fat: 17.3g | Sat Fat: 9.2g | Carbohydrates: 32.9g | Fiber: 0.8g | Sugar: 25.7g | Protein: 4.6g

# Mini Marshmallow Gelato

## Ingredients:

¼ cup mini marshmallows
1 cup whole milk
½ cup heavy cream

¼ cup sugar
3 egg yolks
Pinch of sea salt

## Preparation:

1. Preheat your oven to broiler. 2. Lightly grease a baking sheet. 3. Arrange the marshmallows onto the prepared baking sheet in a single layer. 4. Broil for about 5 minutes, flipping once halfway through. 5. Meanwhile, in a small-sized saucepan, add the milk, heavy cream, sugar, egg yolks and a pinch of salt and whisk until blended thoroughly. 6. Place the saucepan over medium heat and cook for about 1 minute, stirring continuously. 7. Remove the pan of milk mixture from heat and stir in half of the marshmallows. 8. Transfer the mixture into an empty Ninja CREAMi pint container. 9. Place the container into an ice bath to cool. 10. After cooling, cover the container with the storage lid and freeze for 24 hours. 11. Reserve the remaining marshmallows into the freezer. 12. After 24 hours, remove the lid from container and arrange into the outer bowl of Ninja CREAMi. 13. Install the "Creamerizer Paddle" onto the lid of outer bowl. 14. Then rotate the lid clockwise to lock. 15. Press "Power" button to turn on the unit. 16. Then press "GELATO" button. 17. When the program is completed, with a spoon, create a 1½-inch wide hole in the center that reaches the bottom of the pint container. 18. Add the reserved frozen marshmallows into the hole and press "MIX-IN" button. 19. When the program is completed, turn the outer bowl and release it from the machine. 20. Transfer the gelato into serving bowls and serve immediately.

Nutritional Information per Serving: Calories: 186 | Fat: 10.9g | Sat Fat: 2.1g | Carbohydrates: 18.7g | Fiber: 0g | Sugar: 17.6g | Protein: 4.4g

# Vanilla Marshmallow Cookie Gelato

## Ingredients:

1 whole vanilla bean, split in half lengthwise and scraped
4 egg yolks
¾ cup heavy cream
⅓ cup whole milk
2 tablespoons granulated sugar

1 tablespoon light corn syrup
1 teaspoon vanilla extract
5 tablespoons marshmallow paste
5 peanut butter cookies, chopped

## Preparation:

1. In a medium-sized saucepan, add the vanilla bean over medium-high heat, and toast for about 2-3 minutes, stirring continuously. 2. Now, adjust the heat to medium-low and whisk in the egg yolks, heavy cream, milk, sugar, corn syrup, marshmallow paste and vanilla extract. 3. Cook for about 2-3 minutes, stirring continuously. 4. Remove the pan of milk mixture from heat and through a fine-mesh strainer, strain the mixture into an empty Ninja CREAMi pint container. 5. Place the container into an ice bath to cool. 6. After cooling, cover the container with the storage lid and freeze for 24 hours. 7. After 24 hours, remove the lid from container and arrange into the outer bowl of Ninja CREAMi. 8. Install the "Creamerizer Paddle" onto the lid of outer bowl. 9. Then rotate the lid clockwise to lock. Press "Power" button to turn on the unit. 10. Then press "GELATO" button. 11. When the program is completed, with a spoon, create a 1½-inch wide hole in the center that reaches the bottom of the pint container. 12. Add the cookies into the hole and press "MIX-IN" button. 13. When the program is completed, turn the outer bowl and release it from the machine. 14. Transfer the gelato into serving bowls and serve immediately.

**Nutritional Information per Serving:** Calories: 345 | Fat: 21g | Sat Fat: 4.3g | Carbohydrates: 31.9g | Fiber: 1.3g | Sugar: 21.1g | Protein: 6.3g

# Conclusion

Whether it's the ice creams, smoothies, milkshakes, or sorbets, with Ninja Creami, you can make them all with perfection. The machine has the name Creami for no other reason, it does make the creamiest delights you will ever come across, but to achieve such results, you will have to follow the recipes I have shared in this cookbook and stick to the instructions shared here. You can also make use of the recipes and instructions that come with the appliance to better understand the machine. And once you do, you can create your own variety of frozen desserts with your favorite flavors and toppings.

# Appendix 1 Measurement Conversion Chart

## VOLUME EQUIVALENTS (LIQUID)

| US STANDARD | US STANDARD (OUNCES) | METRIC (APPROXIMATE) |
|---|---|---|
| 2 tablespoons | 1 fl.oz | 30 mL |
| ¼ cup | 2 fl.oz | 60 mL |
| ½ cup | 4 fl.oz | 120 mL |
| 1 cup | 8 fl.oz | 240 mL |
| 1½ cup | 12 fl.oz | 355 mL |
| 2 cups or 1 pint | 16 fl.oz | 475 mL |
| 4 cups or 1 quart | 32 fl.oz | 1 L |
| 1 gallon | 128 fl.oz | 4 L |

## VOLUME EQUIVALENTS (DRY)

| US STANDARD | METRIC (APPROXIMATE) |
|---|---|
| ⅛ teaspoon | 0.5 mL |
| ¼ teaspoon | 1 mL |
| ½ teaspoon | 2 mL |
| ¾ teaspoon | 4 mL |
| 1 teaspoon | 5 mL |
| 1 tablespoon | 15 mL |
| ¼ cup | 59 mL |
| ½ cup | 118 mL |
| ¾ cup | 177 mL |
| 1 cup | 235 mL |
| 2 cups | 475 mL |
| 3 cups | 700 mL |
| 4 cups | 1 L |

## TEMPERATURES EQUIVALENTS

| FAHRENHEIT(F) | CELSIUS（C）(APPROXIMATE) |
|---|---|
| 225 °F | 107 °C |
| 250 °F | 120 °C |
| 275 °F | 135 °C |
| 300 °F | 150 °C |
| 325 °F | 160 °C |
| 350 °F | 180 °C |
| 375 °F | 190 °C |
| 400 °F | 205 °C |
| 425 °F | 220 °C |
| 450 °F | 235 °C |
| 475 °F | 245 °C |
| 500 °F | 260 °C |

## WEIGHT EQUIVALENTS

| US STANDARD | METRIC (APPROXINATE) |
|---|---|
| 1 ounce | 28 g |
| 2 ounces | 57 g |
| 5 ounces | 142 g |
| 10 ounces | 284 g |
| 15 ounces | 425 g |
| 16 ounces (1 pound) | 455 g |
| 1.5pounds | 680 g |
| 2pounds | 907 g |

# Appendix 2 Recipes Index

Made in the USA
Columbia, SC
21 December 2024

50410209R00067